India and Global Crisis

SHANKAR ACHARYA is one of India's leading policy economists. As Chief Economic Adviser to the Government of India (1993-2000) he was deeply involved in the economic reforms of the 1990s. He also served on the Securities and Exchange Board of India (SEBI) and, more recently, as Member, Twelfth Finance Commission (2004). He has authored six books and numerous scholarly articles.

Currently he is Honorary Professor and Board Member of the Indian Council for Research on International Economic Relations (ICRIER), New Delhi. He also serves on the governing boards of other national research organisations and various advisory bodies of Government, the Reserve Bank and some corporates. He writes regularly in the Business Standard, and is a consultant to international organisations. Dr. Acharya has a Ph.D. from Harvard University and a B.A. from Oxford.

India and Global Crisis

Shankar Acharya

ACADEMIC FOUNDATION
NEW DELHI

First published in 2009
by

ACADEMIC FOUNDATION
4772-73 / 23 Bharat Ram Road, (23 Ansari Road),
Darya Ganj, New Delhi - 110 002 (India).
Phones : 23245001 / 02 / 03 / 04.
Fax : +91-11-23245005.
E-mail : academic@vsnl.com
www. academicfoundation.com

Cataloging in Publication Data--DK
Courtesy: D.K. Agencies (P) Ltd. <docinfo@dkagencies.com>

Acharya, Shankar N. (Shankar Nath), 1921-
India and global crisis/Shankar Acharya.
p. cm.
Articles; some previously published.
ISBN 13: 9788171887507
ISBN 10: 8171887503

1. Financial crises. 2. International economic relations. 3. Economic development--India. 4. India--Economic policy--1991- I. Title.

DDC 338.954 22

Typeset by Italics India, New Delhi.
Printed and bound in India.

10 9 8 7 6 5 4 3 2 1

In memory of my parents, Bejoy and Nilima, who taught me to read, write and think

Contents

IV. Financial Sector

V. Fiscal Policy

VI. Employment and Inequality

VII. General

Preface

As 2008 comes to a close, the world economy is being buffeted by the worst financial and economic crisis since the Great Depression of the 1930s. The United States, Europe and Japan, the three largest economies in the world, are already in recession. That is, they have experienced a second successive quarter of negative economic growth. International financial markets are still dysfunctional, despite trillions of dollars pumped in by major governments and their central banks to bail out failing banks and attempt to "unfreeze" credit markets. In the large emerging countries (Brazil, Russia, India, and China) also, stock markets have crashed, liquidity is tight, and growth is decelerating sharply. The outlook is bleak, with substantial likelihood of a prolonged slump in industrial countries and slow growth in developing nations. Uncertainty and fear are taking a large toll of output, investment and employment. Poverty and unemployment are rising worldwide.

The current crisis has been several years in the making. And the causes are multiple. They include: the prolonged housing boom in the US (and some European countries) and the growing practice of "sub-prime" lending; the massive balance of payments deficits of the US, whether due to excess spending in America or a "savings glut" in Asia and oil-exporting countries; the many years of easy monetary policy in the US; the sustained borrowing binge in America and unsustainably high ratios of debt to income; the proliferation of opaque financial derivatives, which spread the risks of dodgy mortgage (and other) loans throughout the financial system of industrial countries; the failure (again) of major credit rating agencies which assigned AAA ratings to complex debt securities of dubious quality; enormous weaknesses in financial regulation in America, fostered by the aggressive free market ideology of the Bush years; and simple, unchecked greed.

The unravelling of the house of financial cards began in the winter of 2006/07, when house prices in America began to fall. By the summer of 2007 financial stress had spread widely, with some mortgage banks and hedge funds going under. By autumn, major US and European financial institutions were revealing huge losses due to their exposure to mortgage-backed securities. In September 2007, the UK's Northern Rock bank suffered a run and had to be bailed out by the government and central bank. In March 2008, Bear Stearns, the fifth largest US investment bank, ceased to exist. As doubts and fears about financial viability of major banks mounted and credit became scarce, central banks in the US, the UK and Europe loosened monetary policy sharply and pumped in hundreds of billions of dollars in liquidity. After a seeming lull, financial anxieties deepened gravely and exploded in September 2008, when the US Fed and Treasury had to organise massive bail-outs and buyouts for the giant, government-sponsored mortgage finance institutions, Fannie Mae and Freddie Mac, the iconic investment bank Merrill Lynch and the world's largest insurance company, AIG. On September 15, in a huge policy error, the fourth largest American investment bank, Lehman Brothers, was allowed to topple into bankruptcy. Credit markets across industrial countries froze and transmitted the liquidity shock across the entire world. Since then, there have been further massive bail-outs and bank recapitalisations by the US and European authorities but they have neither revived the financial markets nor stemmed the deepening slide in the global economy since spring 2008.

In India, right up through the summer of 2008, the mounting global financial crisis was largely viewed as a rich country problem, with little direct relevance for major emerging nations like India, except for the big slump in bloated stock market prices, which began in January 2008. 'Decoupling' was still a fashionable theory, which maintained that developing countries could retain their high growth momentum, despite a sharp slowdown in the industrial world. Indeed, in the spring and summer of 2008, Indian economic policy was much more preoccupied with a by-product of the global economic boom of 2002-2007, namely, the massive spike in oil and other commodity prices, which more than doubled India's rate of inflation between March and June 2008 and triggered a significant tightening of monetary policy. The implosion of the US and European financial markets in September 2008 shattered the 'decoupling' myth. The ensuing liquidity shock amplified greatly the already extant trends of slowdown in the growth of industry and services and, together with the abrupt drop in exports in October, knocked the stuffing out of the five-year-old investment boom. Suddenly, the deflationary shocks emanating from global crisis were all too palpable in India as output, investment and employment fell in a growing number of sectors.

Against this background, it is not surprising that the first seven items in this collection of columns from the *Business Standard* (plus a couple from *Outlook*), published between December 2006 and December 2008, deal with different facets of the global financial crisis as it unfolded. In the first, penned in January 2008, the Indian economic boom is still in full swing, though some stresses and strains are becoming apparent. In the last four essays in Section I, the focus is squarely on the global crisis, its impact on India and the scope for remedial policies. The recent sharp declines in output of key sectors (such as steel, automobiles, commercial vehicles, construction, finance and real estate) suggests that it is quite possible for economic growth in 2008/09 to dip below 7 per cent. More importantly, economic activity in the next year or two is destined to remain subdued, with growth in 2009/10 likely to drop below 6 per cent.

Section II deals with macroeconomic policies. Several of the essays highlight the critical importance of maintaining a competitive exchange rate, especially when a multi-year surge in foreign capital inflows threatens to appreciate the rupee's value to uncompetitive levels. In retrospect, we are extremely fortunate that the Reserve Bank demonstrated much courage and independence in limiting exchange rate appreciation in the boom years 2003-2007 and building up foreign exchange reserves of over $ 300 billion. But for these policies we would now be witnessing far more damaging exchange rate volatility and, possibly, a full fledged currency crisis.

The next section comprises essays on the hardy perennial of economic growth. Is it being measured correctly? What are its main causes? What are the key constraints? How strong was the upswing in manufacturing? The last essay in this section reminds us that that the five years between April 2003 and March 2008 was a truly exceptional quinquennium for Indian macroeconomic performance. Growth was at its fastest, inflation at its lowest, external payments most comfortable, fiscal deficits declining and domestic savings and investment surging to new peaks. How soon can we recapture those halcyon years?

Section IV takes up financial sector issues, on which the government issued two major expert committee reports: the first on "Mumbai as an International Financial Centre" (MIFC) in spring 2007 and the second, chaired by professor Raghuram Rajan of Chicago University business school, on the overall financial sector in summer 2008. While both these reports contained useful information and analysis, they also had major flaws which are highlighted by the essays in this section. For example, the MIFC report recommended full capital account convertibility for India by spring 2008. Had the government actually implemented that recommendation, the Indian economy would have suffered enormous damage from the current global financial turmoil. Another essay points to how the current global financial crisis has undermined the three pillars of the "New Orthodoxy": an independent central bank, sole objective of inflation targeting and a single financial regulator.

The essays in the next section return to another hardy perennial, fiscal policy. Two of the essays critically appraise the Chidambaram budgets of 2007 and 2008. Another warns of the fiscal consequences of the Sixth Pay Commission. A fourth critiques the growing prevalence of oil bonds (and other off budget expenditure items) to thinly disguise massive subsidies on oil and other products. Such practices do not blunt the adverse fiscal and economic consequences of large subsidies. They also run the risk of major supply disruptions arising from cash shortages plaguing government oil marketing companies. The fifth essay reminds us of the huge costs being paid by the Indian economy because of continuing large subsidies for electricity, irrigation, urban water supply and higher education.

Section VI takes up longer term, structural issues of rising inequality in India, massive inadequacies in the health sector and the slow growth of jobs, thanks to the highly anti-new-employment labour laws, which bedevil India's labour markets. The enormity of income inequality is brought out by the fact that some recent management graduates earn Rs. 10,000 a day, while in parts of India, farmers struggle to earn the same amount in a whole year. Such glaring inequalities are perpetuated by huge failures in health and nutrition which lead to 46 per cent of children (under 3 years) of India being underweight and nearly 80 per cent being anaemic. The problems of inequality are greatly worsened by our rigid labour laws, which hugely discourage fresh employment in the organised sector of the economy. Indeed, in the absence of serious reform of such laws, the much-touted "demographic dividend" of a young population could rapidly transform into an unemployment nightmare, especially if the global economic crisis condemns India to an extended period of slow economic growth.

The essays in the final section cover a range of general topics, including: the continued (and overwhelming) dominance of China in comparison with India; the UPA government's weak economic legacy; the prime minister's astonishing success in pulling off the civilian nuclear deal with the US in the face of massive odds; and the long term social and political significance of Barack Obama's election.

Finally, I am very grateful to the *Business Standard* and *Outlook* for permission to include in this volume articles originally published in these excellent journals. I am also indebted to Academic Foundation, especially Rituraj Kapila, for maintaining their usual high standards of speed, accuracy and quality in transforming a manuscript into a book. Above all, I want to thank all my readers for their constant encouragement and supportive feedback.

Shankar Acharya

December 2008

I

Global Crisis and India

1 Chasm at Our Feet

2007 rang in the fifth consecutive year of strong economic growth in India, averaging over 8 per cent a year. Domestic savings and investment boomed, corporate profits grew fat, the Sensex surged more than 6000 points to breach 20,000 and real estate prices soared to new highs. Reflecting India Inc's new-found strength, Tata Steel bought out the Corus Group. Billionaires proliferated and there was a *crorepati* around every street corner. Salaries jumped. Eighty million more cell phones jangled. A million more cars choked the pot-holed roads and their exhaust fumes clouded the skies over urban India and challenged the respiratory capacities of residents. The shopping malls got bigger, the weddings glitzier, the magazines glossier and the movies raunchier. Domestic air travel spiked up by 40 per cent and nearly 10 million Indians went abroad for business or pleasure. Yes, the boom times continued, at least in urban India.

But for every million new entrants to India's burgeoning middle class there were tens of millions of citizens still trapped in grinding rural poverty, lucky to earn 10,000 rupees a year (yes, a year) through back-breaking labour. For them, there was no party. Electricity was still a rare luxury, roads were mostly non-existent, water sources were usually contaminated, crops still failed and "law and justice" were cruel jokes. Worse, the hopes of escaping poverty remained fragile, with abysmal standards of teaching in most government schools and few job opportunities for school leavers and dropouts. In a word, the abyss between boom-time, metropolitan India and rural Bharat widened further during 2007.

Let's not dwell on the downside. The fact is that fifth year running of strong economic growth was a real achievement and reflected several key trends, including: the cumulative impact of 15 years of economic reform (though not much by the present government); the rewards of opening up to global commerce and capital; the coming of age of India's dynamic corporate sector; the savings dividend of a young labour force; the impetus from modern services such as IT, telecom and media; a competitive exchange rate policy (till this spring); some reduction of fiscal deficits; and an unprecedented global economic boom. Across the world there was increasing recognition and respect for India's recent economic performance and future potential.

The year began with inflation jitters, which were skillfully soothed through a modulated tightening of monetary policy by the RBI. However, food prices continued to rise, driven by global scarcities and longer-term weaknesses in domestic agricultural supply. The booming Indian economy attracted a rising tide of foreign capital inflows as domestic companies borrowed liberally from overseas lenders and foreign investors piled into the country's buoyant stock markets. This surge in external capital and an apparent shift in government policy led to a sharp and unexpected jump of more than 10 per cent in the rupee/dollar rate exchange in March-April. The adverse impact on the nation's exports (especially in employment-intensive segments like textiles, leather goods and handicrafts) followed in a few months and intensified, destroying hundreds of thousands of manufacturing jobs, weakening the boom in software exports and posing a serious (and still unresolved) dilemma for policy-makers and politicians.

Foreign capital inflows were not the only marker of India's growing integration with the world economy. As global oil prices soared from an already high $60/barrel in January to nearly $100 in November, India's trade deficit widened by $ 15 billion and the pressure to raise domestic prices oil products intensified. Confronted by populist, Left-led opposition to oil price increases, the UPA government chose to pass most of the burden of the surging subsidies (on petrol, diesel and LPG) on to the domestic oil companies, severely undermining their financial health and capacity for investing in domestic supply expansion. Efforts to reduce the country's growing, long-term dependence on costly imported petroleum through more reliance on nuclear power were dealt a massive setback by the Left's pulling the rug from under the Indo-US nuclear deal in October. The widening political rift between the UPA and the Left ramped up political uncertainty and preponed the likely date of the next general election.

From August onwards the global economy cast another lengthening shadow on India's ongoing growth surge. The "sub-prime" mortgage lending problems in the US housing market snowballed into a global credit crunch in the industrial world as it became increasingly apparent that lenders of these dodgy mortgages had transferred the underlying credit risks to numerous banks and other financial firms through complex and opaque financial "innovations". By October, blue-chip financial giants like Citibank and Merrill Lynch were declaring billions in losses from these activities and credit markets in the US, Europe and Japan were in a deep funk. While the short-term fallout for India and other Asian economies was limited, the chances of some growth retardation in 2008 and beyond rose by the month, in tandem with the rising probability of a recession in the US. Although the jury is still out on severity of the impact on the US economy of the collapse in home construction and a stalled financial industry, most respected analysts expect a significant slowdown, if not a deep recession. And if the six-year long US economic expansion cools, the rest of the world, including India, will surely feel the chill ("decoupling" theories notwithstanding).

Global uncertainties are not the only clouds darkening the prospects for sustaining India's current nine per cent growth momentum. Unresolved problems and stalled reforms could also spoil the party. Long-standing infrastructure bottlenecks in power, roads, water supply and urban services may exact a rising toll from the growth festivities. The recent and hard-won gains in fiscal prudence could be blown off course by the growing recourse to off-budget subsidies (for oil, food and fertiliser), the ticking time-bomb of the Sixth Pay Commission, mounting expenditure on populist programmes or a slackening of the recent surge in corporate profits and taxes. The well-known failures in government education and health systems are impeding the development of the human resources so essential for sustaining rapid economic and social development. Agricultural performance remains well below potential and is unlikely to meet the Eleventh Plan target of four per cent growth without major reforms. Continued government ownership of the commanding heights in banking and energy could also hurt future development.

Perhaps most worrying for the long-run are the increasing dualisms between rich *versus* poor, organised *versus* informal sectors, urban *versus* rural, employed *versus* jobless, fast-growing *versus* backward regions and skilled *versus* unskilled labour. The party may still be swinging....but it's not for everybody. How long before the widening economic and social disparities fuel serious social strife, which shreds the remnants of reasonable governance and impedes the overall momentum of development?

Outlook, January 14, 2008.

2 The Darkening Sky

How things change in three months. Back in early March, India's economic growth was still barreling along at around nine per cent. Headline inflation data (for late February) still indicated a "comfortable" five per cent rate. The finance minister, fresh from presenting a populist budget, was confidently projecting the continuation of a "9 per cent batting average" on growth. The sub-prime credit crunch in industrial countries seemed to have little direct fallout for India and the indirect effects through slower OECD growth were as yet distant. True, international oil prices had broken the talismanic $100/bbl level but concern in India was muted, mainly because domestic prices were held unchanged and the fiscal burden of massive implicit subsidies was masked by the double ploys of hammering oil company profits and issuing oil bonds. True, some economists had carped about a fiscally lax budget (including unfunded subsidies for oil, fertilisers and food), lack of reform and the damage to the credit culture from the farm loan waiver. But hey, who listens to economists? The overall mood remained quite buoyant.

Three months later things look much less rosy. The indicators of slowing growth proliferate in the daily papers. The government and RBI are in a small minority in expecting growth in 2008/09 to attain 8.5 to 9 per cent. The great majority of independent analysts expect the outcome to be in the 7 to 8 per cent range, with a growing number favouring the lower side of this band. Equity markets have tanked and stock prices are in doldrums. The really nasty surprise has come from inflation. Headline inflation has shot up since March and stood at a very uncomfortable 11 per cent in early June. Although a whole slew of fiscal, monetary and administrative measures have been deployed by the authorities, there is little respite in sight. The price spike has been concentrated in commodities, especially food, metals, fertilisers, and oil products (either uncontrolled or because of rare upward revisions in controlled prices of petrol, diesel, kerosene, and LPG). Yes, the primary source of this inflationary surge has been external, but that provides little consolation to people buying goods and services.

The other great dampener to economic spirits has been the growing realisation that the fiscal situation has suddenly turned quite dire. The February budget's estimate of a Central government deficit of 2.5 per cent of GDP for 2008/09 appears laughably optimistic. As fuel, fertiliser, and food prices soared since March and the corresponding "issue" or user prices were kept unchanged by the government, the estimates of implicit subsidies on these items rose steeply: over three per cent of GDP on fuel; nearly two per cent on fertilisers, and perhaps one per cent on food. Even allowing for revenue increases on higher rupee bases, a true (implicit subsidy inclusive) central fiscal deficit of around 6 to 7 per cent of GDP seemed very likely. Together with the State fiscal deficits in the order of 2 to 3 per cent of GDP, the combined true fiscal deficit is clearly going to be in the range of 9 to 10 per cent of GDP. Keeping these true deficits off the budget books through devices such as oil bonds and arrears owed to public entities in food and fertiliser in no way dilutes their adverse economic consequences. Nor does it fool knowledgeable observers. By April and May, more and more analysts and investment banks were routinely reporting such high deficits, making a mockery of the budget estimate and (more importantly) pointing to a correspondingly heavier public sector borrowing burden on the market for loanable funds and hardening interest rates.

The drivers behind the burgeoning fiscal deficit have been the surging international prices of oil, fertilisers, and food. The same factors are causing the yawning deficits in foreign trade and the current account of the balance of payments. If world oil prices average around $ 130/bbl in 2008/09, India's commodity trade deficit is likely to be in the order of 10 per cent of GDP and the current account deficit close to 4 per cent of GDP. (Very roughly, every $2/bbl change in the average world oil price means a 0.1 per cent of GDP change in the current account deficit.) Unsurprisingly, the five year old problem of external capital surge seems to have disappeared, with the current account deficit widening and FIIs withdrawing over $ 5 billion from Indian capital markets in the first five months of 2008. Suddenly, it seems more like 1987-1990, with reforms stalled, fiscal and balance of payment deficits ballooning, and political uncertainty on the rise.

Actually, of course, things are not nearly as bad as the late 1980s for three important reasons. First, the RBI holds more than $ 300 billion of foreign exchange reserves as insurance against temporary liquidity crunches on external account. A couple of years of balance of payments strain could be absorbed easily without undue turmoil in external trade and payments. Second, the Indian private sector is in far better shape today than 20 years ago on all the usual yardsticks of productivity, profitability, balance sheet strength and dynamism. In theory, at least, it is much better placed to ride out temporary stresses in the economic environment. Third, the latest official data indicate that aggregate investment in the economy was 41 per cent of GDP in 2007/08. It would be quite unlikely to drop by more than 6 or 7 per cent of GDP even if the economy goes through a couple of weak years. That suggests aggregate investment levels will probably not fall below 34-35 per cent of GDP, which, in turn, makes economic growth below 7 per cent a year somewhat unlikely. However, given the massive scale of the implicit subsidies noted above, a deterioration in public savings of 4 to 5 per cent of GDP is quite possible, associated with a drop in investment and a widening of the investment-savings gap.

The trajectory of corporate investment and savings (which have risen sharply in recent years) is much more uncertain. The exceptionally difficult short-term challenge for monetary policy will be to contain the current, strong inflationary tendencies and expectations without inflicting undue damage to private investment. We know that in 2008/09 the investment-savings gap may need to widen by perhaps 2 per cent of GDP to accommodate the higher current account deficit. The question is at what level (of total savings and investment) will the equilibration occur. Beyond the short-run, fiscal policy (including price increases of fuel, fertiliser, and food) must shoulder the primary responsibility for reducing macro imbalances.

Seven months ago (*Business Standard*, November 22, 2007) I wrote, "the UPA's legacy for sustaining rapid and inclusive growth in future years leaves a lot to be desired." Since then, the government's continued and prolonged failure to gradually adjust domestic oil prices to international realities has spawned a massive fiscal deficit and significantly worsened this government's already dubious economic legacy.

Business Standard, June 26, 2008.

3 The Triple Punch

The world economy enjoyed an exceptionally strong (and wholly unexpected) boom in the period 2002-2007 with global growth averaging about five per cent a year. It was no coincidence that India's record five-year growth at nearly nine per cent a year occurred in 2003/04-2007/08. If anyone needed further proof of the wisdom of India's "opening up to the world" policies of the 1990s and beyond, it would be hard to find a stronger vindication. While domestic factors (such as surging savings/investment, a services boom and the cumulative effects of earlier reforms) probably played the dominant role in driving India's growth acceleration, the benign international environment of strong trade expansion and burgeoning cross-border flows of capital and technology undoubtedly played a significant part. But globalisation cannot be a bed of roses. There are bound to be some thorns. When the world economy runs into rough weather, participant countries can expect some pain. In 2008, the combination of the global credit crunch and the steep rise in international commodity prices (especially oil) has dealt India a triple punch: through plummeting stock prices, an unprecedented spurt in inflation, and slower growth.

The blow to equity prices came first, beginning January 2008. A potent brew of souring global equity markets and a reassessment (by investors) of the oil-import-dependent Indian economy sent the Sensex tumbling down 40 per cent from the inflated levels of mid-January. The second big punch landed in March 2008, as soaring prices of oil, food (especially edible oils) and metals transformed a "comfortable" inflation rate of around 5 per cent to an extremely painful 12 per cent rate in four short months. This has been the sharpest rise in headline inflation experienced by the country since Independence. It may also have been the least anticipated. Basically, the global economy has delivered a terms-of-trade shock to which the Indian economy and policies have to adjust. Some of the price shock may correct over time as the global commodity price boom subsides. But it is unlikely that international oil prices will revert below $80/bbl or that fertiliser prices will return to pre-2008 levels. The enduring part of the price shock poses significant challenges to fiscal, monetary, price and exchange rate policies as part of the necessary adjustment to permanently elevated relative prices of key commodities. It also implies an inevitable, though hopefully temporary, decline in the country's growth rate.

The third punch, to economic growth, has not yet been fully delivered. Yes, the commodity price shock has already begun to take its toll of growth momentum. But that's only part of the blow to growth. In fact, the price surge was a by-product of the strong global boom. What has yet to hit India is the full weight of the post-boom slowdown in the global economy. This point may not be adequately appreciated in India for three reasons. First, there is a belief that the "sub-prime" related global credit crunch is now past its worst point and financial market recovery is under way. Second, despite the global deceleration, India's exports grew at a healthy 22 per cent (in dollars) in April-June 2008. So where's the worry? Third, surely the penalty in the form of slower growth is already accounted for in the various downward-revised growth projections for the Indian economy in 2008/09. For example, the RBI has trimmed its projection to 8 per cent; CRISIL has reduced its forecast down to 7.8 per cent (from an earlier 8.5 per cent); NCAER has dropped it to 7.8 per cent (from its earlier 8.5-8.8 per cent range) and JP Morgan to 7.0 per cent (from 7.5 per cent). Some of these projections look quite optimistic now that data for industrial production shows growth of only 5.2 per cent in the April-June quarter of 2008, compared to 10.3 per cent in the previous year. Besides, it's 2009/10 that I would worry about more, for reasons outlined below.

To elaborate on the first point, every passing quarter suggests that the severity of the financial market problems (that emerged a year ago) and their adverse impact on national output in the US and Europe is likely to be greater than originally expected. As former US Treasury Secretary, Lawrence Summers puts it (*Financial Times*, August 7, 2008): "There is growing consensus that the west is facing the most serious financial crisis since the second world war...Four vicious cycles are simultaneously under way: falling asset prices are forcing levered holders to sell, driving prices further down; losses at financial institutions are reducing their ability to finance investment, which in turn reduces asset values, causing further losses; the weakness of the financial system is reducing growth, which in turn weakens the financial system; and falling output is hitting employment, which in turn reduces demand for output." Summers estimates that "the American economy is operating between 2 and 2.5 per cent below its sustainable potential level." Worse, he expects further slowing of the US growth could lead to a near doubling of this gap in the next year or so. Recent reports indicate that growth in Europe and Japan is also slowing more than earlier expected. Asia's trade-dependent economies will undoubtedly suffer from this slowdown in US-Europe-Japan. India's growth cannot be immune to these developments, no matter what the recent export data show (which are any way inflated by petroleum exports from a couple of private refineries).

So, the world economy's punch to Indian growth has not yet landed with full force. It will have done so by 2009. Add to that the other growth-retarding factors that are in play already, including: the higher interest rates from tightened monetary policy (perhaps the July measures were excessive) and much higher government borrowing because of huge subsidies on oil, fertiliser, and food; the likely decline in savings and investment in 2008/09 (see my piece in *Business Standard,* June 26, 2008); the negative effects of four years of "pause" in economic reforms; the downturn in the business cycle in industry; and the over-reliance on monetary policy to cope with the recent terms of trade shock. All things considered, it should not be a surprise if India's economic growth dips below 7 per cent in 2009/10. Of course, much will depend on the uncertain trajectory of international oil prices.

Business Standard, August 14, 2008.

4 Crisis and Response

If you don't know what a CDO (collateralised debt obligation) or a CDS (credit default swap) is, don't worry. Nor does 99.9999 per cent of the US populace, which will soon vote for its next President in the midst of the biggest financial crisis since 1929. These acronyms refer to some opaque financial instruments, which have spread the contagion of billions of dollars of "sub-prime" (meaning "very risky") mortgage loans in the US throughout that country's financial system and to much of the industrial world. With the US house prices falling over the last 18 months and sub-prime mortgages going sour, these CDOs and CDSs have wrought havoc on the US financial industry. Wall Street, as we knew it, no longer exists. The crisis, which has been simmering since July 2007, came to a boil this month.

On September 7th, the US government conducted a bail-out and *de facto* nationalisation of the giant, government-sponsored (but privately owned) mortgage financiers, Fannie Mae and Freddie Mac. The following Sunday, Lehman Brothers, the fourth largest investment bank, toppled into bankruptcy, while Merrill Lynch (the third largest) was bought out by Bank of America. On the 17th (a weekday for a change) the "dynamic duo" of Treasury's Paulson and Fed's Bernanke carried out a bail-out and quasi-nationalisation of the world's largest insurance firm, AIG. Last Sunday, the 21st, the Fed engineered the transformation of the two remaining (and largest) investment banks, Morgan Stanley and Goldman Sachs, into bank holding companies, thereby ensuring that stand alone investment banks joined dinosaurs in the march of evolution. Over the weekend the US government also unveiled a $700 billion rescue fund aimed at detoxifying the US financial industry by buying out its "troubled assets".

This unprecedented and ongoing global financial crisis will have many lessons and consequences for India, most of which are currently obscured by the fog of financial destruction and upheaval still under way. Let me point to a few. First, the hugely varied and heterodox responses of the US authorities (especially Treasury and Fed) have been remarkable. The actions have encompassed deep interest rate cuts, massive liquidity injections, ban on short selling, managed buyouts of ailing giants (Bear Stearns and Merrill), allowing bankruptcy (Lehman), *de facto* nationalisations (Fanny Mae, Freddie

Mac and AIG), guarantee of money market fund accounts and now the newly proposed "bail-out fund". Textbook dicta against "moral hazard" and central bank lending to non-banks have been ignored. In the face of financial meltdown, pragmatism has been the order of the day. Two principles seem to have guided these policies: let markets punish shareholders of the failing institutions, but bail-out those posing high systemic risk. The policy responses adopted by Paulson, Bernanke, Geithner and Cox will be debated for decades. It is a reasonable prediction that our local finance ayatollahs will applaud their heterodox approach. It would have been nice if they had been equally charitable to the heterodox and largely successful policy response of the RBI to the unprecedented foreign capital surge experienced by India in 2003-2007.

Second, the speed and apparent effectiveness of coordination between the Treasury, Fed, SEC, and others has been impressive. Note that this has been achieved without any formal structure such as the Financial Sector Oversight Agency (FSOA) recommended for India by the Raghuram Rajan report. This vindicates my earlier expressed doubts (*Business Standard*, April 10, 2008) about the wisdom of an FSOA. What matters is the quality and knowledge of the people at the helm, not the bureaucratic structures. On this score we need to worry, following the recent departures of top-notch policy administrators/ advisers ex-Governor Reddy and ex-EAC Chairman Rangarajan. Their replacements are able people but still lacking in financial domain knowledge. The situation will worsen with the likely exit of RBI Deputy Governor Rakesh Mohan, currently the person with the greatest money/finance domain knowledge in the *sarkari* system.

What are some likely implications of this global crisis for India? First, thanks to Reddy's policies, the Indian banking system is well-capitalised and has very little exposure to the toxic instruments swilling around in international finance. Second, again thanks to him, the RBI is armed with nearly $ 300 billion of forex reserves, more than enough to ride out the inevitable drop in capital inflows (in 2008, through August, about a billion dollars a month net have been withdrawn by FIIs as they strove to shore up their capital positions in home jurisdictions). Third, faced by a short-term surge in capital outflows the correct policy (already in place) is for the RBI to allow some downward flexibility of the nominal exchange rate, while keeping the "brakes on" through dollar sales. The wrong policies would be to try and defend a particular nominal rate or to signal panic by suddenly liberalising guidelines for external commercial borrowing or relaxing the norms for Participatory Notes (good KYC norms are especially pertinent at the present highly uncertain juncture).

Fourth, this is obviously the wrong time for further capital account liberalisation, with the merchandise trade deficit running at around 10 per cent of GDP, rebounding oil prices, a rising fiscal deficit and likely weakening of goods and software exports (this last is extremely likely as the effects of the global financial crisis increasingly stall economic activity in industrial countries and thereby dampen the growth of international trade). It is also important to avoid restrictions on the current account (such as tighter time limits on export proceeds repatriation), since these could end up disrupting trade and normal current transactions.

Fifth, as the world economy inevitably slows and transmits a deflationary impulse to India over the next year or two, our monetary policy will need to be calibrated accordingly to avoid any steep and prolonged decline in investment and economic growth. The deflationary impulse has already been under way but could gain significant momentum from the recent financial drama in the US.

Finally, against this background of inevitable, if temporary, deceleration in global and Indian economic growth, it is very important to avoid other big blows to domestic economic confidence, such as through possible disruptions in country-wide oil supplies triggered by cash shortages in government oil marketing companies. It would be wiser to give these companies subsidies directly (if prices can't be raised) rather than through roundabout and tardy devices like oil bonds (see my piece in *Business Standard*, May 22, 2008). In any case, the fiscal and economic impacts are very similar.

This story is far from over. Its consequences and lessons will be with us for a long time to come.

Table 4.1

Commitment of US Public Funds in the Financial Crisis ($ billion)*

Date	*Institution/Activity*	*Amount*
March 17, 2008	Fed guarantee for J.P. Morgan takeover of Bear Stearns	29.0
September 7, 2008	Treasury bail-out of Fannie Mae and Freddie Mac	200.0
September 17, 2008	Treasury –Fed bail-out of AIG	85.0
September 22, 2008	Treasury Plan for bail-out of "troubled assets"	700.0
Total (up to September 22, 2008)		1014.0

Note: * Excludes several hundred billion dollars of temporary credit extended by Fed to banks and non-banks, some of which may entail losses on "junk" collateral.

Business Standard, September 25, 2008.

5 Coping with Crisis

The global financial crisis, which had been simmering for over a year, came to a boil in September 2008 when major US and European financial institutions teetered on the brink of collapse and had to be bailed out by their respective governments and central banks. In a huge policy error, on September 15, the fourth largest American investment bank, Lehman Brothers, was allowed to go bust and filed for bankruptcy. Almost immediately, Western credit markets froze and massively amplified the recessionary forces at work in the US, Europe and Japan. Since then India and the rest of the world has been coping with the twin global shocks of a worldwide liquidity crunch and deepening global recession. The liquidity shock was immediate, with FII outflows surging, external trade credit vanishing, liabilities of Indian bank branches abroad drying up and needing to be substituted by credit lines from home base and external financing for ambitious foreign acquisitions by Indian corporates disappearing, thus forcing these companies to seek domestic credit. The recessionary shock has begun to hit Indian exports and investment, and will likely intensify in the coming quarters.

How has Indian macroeconomic policy coped with these unprecedented challenges? What more needs to be done? Let us review briefly.

Monetary Policy

After a brief hesitation, the monetary policy response by RBI (and government) has been prompt and substantial. In the sharpest reduction ever, the CRR has been cut from 9 per cent to 5.5 per cent, thus injecting almost Rs. 150,000 crores of primary liquidity in less than a month. In addition, the SLR has been reduced, effectively, to 21.5 per cent (from 25 per cent), with 1.5 per cent points of the reduction earmarked for liquidity support by banks to mutual funds and NBFCs (since some of these entities had been experiencing substantial liquidity stress over the past month). The repo policy rate has been reduced from 9 per cent to 7.5 per cent, effective early November. The RBI has also announced a plethora of other measures to enhance liquidity, liberalise terms for NRI deposits and external commercial borrowing (ECB), augment export credit refinance and (somewhat dubiously) reduce banks' provisioning norms (tightened during the earlier upswing in the credit cycle) for loans for housing, real estate, personal loans, credit card receivables, and capital market exposure.

Despite this major loosening of monetary policy, there is a rising crescendo of demands from industry for more reductions in policy interest rates. In part this reflects the growing severity of the industrial downturn from global shocks; and in part it reflects increasing frustration with the continued high rates at which actual commercial lending and borrowing is taking place. There are at least four reasons why interest rates may not decline very much in the near term. First, even in normal times, the transmission of changes in policy rates to commercial rates is neither swift nor full. In the present environment of high financial stress, transmission is even weaker. Second, the RBI will find it hard to undertake further sharp cuts in both policy rates and the CRR without risking loss of control over an already sliding currency (looser monetary policy usually implies downward pressure on the currency value). Nor is inflation as dead as many assume. The annual rate of CPI (industrial workers) increase was still in uncomfortable double digits in October. Third, given the general (global) scarcity of capital and liquidity and rising stress among borrowers in a sharp slowdown, banks and other financial intermediaries in India will expect higher risk premia from most borrowers (yesterday's AAA client may only look single A today). Finally, the government's record increase in its true fiscal deficit, of over four per cent of GDP via the supplementary demand passed by Parliament last month, points to heavy borrowing requirements from the government sector in the remaining months of the fiscal year.

Fiscal Policy

Additional fiscal stimulus is the global flavour of the season to compensate for declines in exports, investment and consumption demand. Sounds reasonable enough. The only problem is that we in India have already had our fiscal stimulus. Last month the government enacted the largest ever supplementary demand for grants of Rs. 237,286 crores, reflecting a record 33 per cent increase over budget estimates. As Govinda Rao has lucidly detailed (*Business Standard*, November 4, 2008), the bulk of this money has gone to pay for government pay increases, fertiliser subsidy, National Rural Employment

Guarantee Programme spending increases, oil bonds (or postponed oil subsidy), fertiliser bonds (postponed fertiliser subsidy) and the farm loan waiver.

In his interaction with the press on the flight returning from the Washington G20 summit last week, the Prime Minister pretty much implied that the fiscal stimulus for this year was mostly done, though his indication that it had all been anticipated by him and his finance minister at budget time remains a bit implausible. Adding this 4.5 per cent of GDP supplementary to the budgeted fiscal deficit yields a true central fiscal deficit (including off budget items) of 7 per cent of GDP for 2008/09. And this is assuming that there are no further supplementaries and (even more heroically in a sharply slowing economy) that revenue targets are met. Even if an auction of 3G spectrum nets Rs. 30,000 crores in 2008/09, this may only compensate for tax revenue shortfalls. In other words, a consolidated (Centre plus states) fiscal deficit of around 10 per cent of GDP still seems quite likely.

Put simply, we can ill afford further fiscal stimulus in the present year. Perhaps all the huffing and puffing about additional infrastructure spending is designed to boost spending next year, when subsidies for oil and fertilisers may be absent if the currently subdued international commodity prices persist.

Exchange Rate Policy

Since the downward pressure on the rupee started a few months ago, the government and RBI have correctly permitted a controlled slide, backed by substantial RBI forex sales from time to time. (Contrary to popular perception, at least a third of the $ 60 billion drop in reserves is due to valuation changes, according to estimates of various investment banks.) No better alternative policy is available. Defending a particular rupee/$ rate would invite swift and unwanted depletion of reserves. Allowing a "clean float" (no RBI intervention) sounds theoretically appealing until you recall the havoc wrought by such a policy in Indonesia and other East Asian countries a decade ago. The costs of "overshooting" on the downside could be hideously high, both in economic and political terms. So, the only viable policy remains one of intervening selectively and avoiding excessively loose monetary policy.

One other thought: in the months ahead, as the global recession takes its toll of the Indian economy, there may be distress calls for "bail-outs" from various segments of the economy. Each would have its special case. Quite obviously, there may not be enough resources to bail out everyone who seeks help in a growth recession. Selectivity has to be paramount. A good starting point is to consider bail-outs only for those entities whose demise poses systemic risk.

Finally, if the government can forge ahead with economic reforms, it might revive the investment mood. But then, the election season is upon us.

Business Standard, November 27, 2008.

6 Crisis and Growth

The global financial and economic crisis keeps getting worse. A couple of weeks back the giant Citibank had to be bailed out with several hundred billion dollars in cash and guarantees from the US authorities ("Citi never sleeps"... but apparently its management dozed off during some crucial decisions last year). Last week America reported November job losses of more than 530,000, the biggest single month figure since 1974, taking the US unemployment rate to 6.7 per cent, the highest in 15 years. The US, Eurozone, the UK, and Japan are now officially in recession, in the sense of having experienced two successive quarters of negative growth. Several analysts predict that the rate of contraction of the US economy in this final quarter of 2008 may be at an astonishing annual rate of 4 to 5 per cent. Similar pessimism pervades the other two largest economies in the world: Europe and Japan. There is enormous uncertainty about the depth and duration of the current global recession. But the majority of expert opinion now concedes a substantial likelihood that this will be the worst recession since the Great Depression of the 1930s.

Both the severity of the financial crisis and its massive collateral damage to the real economy has confounded the optimists over the past year. Quite often, experts claimed that "the worst of the financial crisis is behind us", only to be bush-whacked by the next big bail-out or credit seizure. Equally remarkable, and much worse in impact, has been the speed at which the cumulating financial crisis has throttled real economic activity since summer 2008. The rapid onset of recession in industrial (advanced) countries has clearly overwhelmed the forecasting abilities of many institutions, including the IMF. As recently as July this year, the IMF foresaw the world economy growing at 3.9 per cent in 2009, advanced economies at 1.4 per cent and developing countries at 6.7 per cent. By early November (just four months later) these forecasts had been slashed down to 2.2 percent, minus 0.3 per cent and 5.1 per cent, respectively (see Table 6.1). For its projections of the US economic growth in 2009, the IMF swung from plus 0.8 per cent in July to minus 0.7 per cent in November! And it's a safe bet that if the IMF were making a fresh set of projections for 2009 today, all these numbers would look even worse.

Nor does the recent "advance release" of the global outlook for 2009 by UNCTAD provide any succour. Like the IMF, the UNCTAD foresees global growth at just over 2 per cent in 2009 at PPP weights and at only 1 per cent at market exchange rates. The latter number means that global growth in 2009 is expected to be at only about a quarter of the pace enjoyed in 2006 and 2007. Both institutions forecast severe damage to world trade, which is expected to expand at only 2 per cent in 2009 as compared to over 9 per cent in 2006 and 7 per cent in 2007. For the Asian giant, China, both the IMF and UNCTAD expect growth to slow to about 8.5 per cent in 2009 from the scorching 12 per cent pace of 2007. Interestingly, several China-based analysts foresee much sharper deceleration.

What about India? How bad will it get for us? The official estimates of GDP growth for the first two quarters of 2008/09 stayed above 7.5 per cent. However, industry-wide indications after September are uniformly gloomy. There are reports of significant declines in output of automobiles, commercial vehicles, steel, textiles, petrochemicals, construction, real estate, finance, retail activity, and many other sectors. Exports fell by 12 per cent in dollar terms in October and advance information points to a similar decline in November. After September, the economy seems almost to have gone over a cliff. When available, the official data are likely to record a sharp slowdown in the second half of the year, possibly steep enough to drag full year growth in 2008/09 to below 7 per cent. What's more, given the strongly recessionary conditions expected to prevail in the world economy in 2009, there is no prospect of a quick turnaround in India. Indeed, on a tentative basis, I would suggest that we might be lucky to achieve GDP growth of even 6 per cent in 2009/10.

What about economic policy? Can we not deploy monetary, fiscal, and exchange rate policies to insulate our growth momentum from adverse external conditions? The short answer is: only to a limited degree. I outlined the main arguments last fortnight (*Business Standard*, November 27). Monetary policy had already been aggressively loosened by early November and the RBI provided a further, well-balanced package last Saturday, notably including a 1 per cent cut in the repo and reverse repo rates. Given the continued high rate of CPI inflation through October (latest data) and, perhaps more significantly, recent pressures on the exchange rate, the present scope for further policy rate reductions appears limited. That situation might change if external imbalances improve if a falling oil import bill and slowing non-oil imports outweigh the drop in export earnings, and if capital flows stabilise.

On the fiscal front, the government had pretty much exhausted the available fiscal space through its record Rs. 237,000 crore (4.5 per cent of GDP) supplementary demand in October. Though undertaken for quite different reasons, its timing may turn out to be quite fortunate. Against this background the government was wise to limit last Sunday's "fiscal stimulus" to a modest affair, totaling only about Rs. 30,000 crores, out of which two-thirds was for "additional plan expenditure", which may not be fully spent this fiscal year. It may be far more important to actually spend the already budgeted plan expenditure effectively. If international oil and fertiliser prices stay at present levels, implying low or negligible subsidy rates (looking ahead) on price-controlled domestic sales, then there may be a case for a larger stimulus next year. Much will depend on the trajectory of revenues and other expenditures in a slowing economy.

While such unprecedented monetary loosening and massive supplementary expenditures will definitely help, they will not fully neutralise the negative impact of the severe global financial and economic crisis on India's exports, investment, and consumption. With over 60 per cent of global GDP having toppled into recession, a significant deceleration of India's economic growth is simply unavoidable. After all, we share the same planet as America, Europe and Japan (and a rapidly slowing China). In this context a 6 per cent economic growth in 2009/10 will be pretty good...if we achieve it.

Business Standard, December 11, 2008.

Table 6.1

IMF and UNCTAD Growth Projections

Annual percentage change

	IMF								UNCTAD	
	2006	2007	2008P		2009P				2008	2009
Month in 2008 when projections made			April	Nov.	April	July	Oct.	Nov.	Dec.	Dec.
World Output[a]	**5.1**	**5.0**	**3.7**	**3.7**	**3.8**	**3.9**	**3.0**	**2.2**	**3.7**	**2.3**
Advanced Economies	**3.0**	**2.6**	**1.3**	**1.4**	**1.3**	**1.4**	**0.5**	**-0.3**	**1.1**	**-0.5**
United States	2.8	2.0	0.5	1.4	0.6	0.8	0.1	-0.7	1.2	-1.0
Euro area	2.8	2.6	1.4	1.2	1.2	1.2	0.2	-0.5	1.1	-0.7
Japan	2.4	2.1	1.4	0.5	1.5	1.5	0.5	-0.2	0.4	-0.3
United Kingdom	2.8	3.0	1.6	0.8	1.6	1.7	-0.1	-1.3	-	-
Emerging and Developing Economies	**7.9**	**8.0**	**6.7**	**6.6**	**6.6**	**6.7**	**6.1**	**5.1**	**6.4[b]**	**4.7[b]**
Russia	7.4	8.1	6.8	6.8	6.3	7.3	5.5	3.5	-	-
China	11.6	11.9	9.3	9.7	9.5	9.8	9.3	8.5	9.1	8.4
India	**9.8**	**9.3**	**7.9**	**7.8**	**8.0**	**8.0**	**6.9**	**6.3**	**7.5**	**7.0**
Brazil	3.8	5.4	4.8	5.2	3.7	4.0	3.5	3.0	5.1	2.9
World growth based on market exchange rates	3.9	3.7	2.6	2.6	2.6	2.7	1.9	1.1	2.5	1.0
World trade volume (goods and services)	**9.4**	**7.2**	**5.6**	**4.6**	**5.8**	**6.0**	**4.1**	**2.1**	**4.4**	**2.1**

Note: a. At purchasing power parity (PPP) weights.

b. Includes " Economies in transition" and " Developing economies."

Sources: www.imf.org and www.unctad.org

7 Tottering BRICs?

Remember "decoupling"? (And I am not referring to mating mammals.) It was that seductive theory which held that the developing world had achieved a high degree of autonomous economic momentum, such that it could sustain fast growth despite any slowdown in the industrial world. Indeed, because of its independent locomotive power, the developing world might even rescue global economic progress from the follies of irresponsible industrial countries. It was particularly odd when some cheerleaders of globalisation became exponents of decoupling. How, one used to ask, could the developing world have reaped the benefits of expanding global trade and capital flows and yet be immune to slumps in these key transmission mechanisms of globalisation? Well, we now have the answer. When two-thirds of the global economy plunges into a serious recession, world trade growth grinds to a halt and net capital inflows to developing countries slump, these nations get hurt badly. The only decoupling is that of romantic theory from hard facts. Even the big boys among developing countries feel the pain. Look what's happening to the mighty BRICs, those much-touted masters of the future. Let's review them in the order of the acronym.

Brazil, the giant of Latin America, was powering along at a y-o-y growth rate of over 6 per cent right up to the third quarter of 2008, fuelled by strong capital inflows and booming exports, which were riding the massive, global commodity boom of the preceding year. By September, the commodity boom was collapsing and the global financial market seizure wreaked havoc on net capital inflows and suddenly throttled domestic liquidity. As these shocks took their toll, Brazil's economy may have actually shrunk in the final quarter of 2008 according to some estimates. The forecasts for economic growth in 2009 are subdued. Goldman Sachs projects it as low as 1.5 per cent (Table 7.1). Obviously, the outcome will depend hugely on developments in world trade and capital flows, both of which are clouded by enormous uncertainty.

As the *Financial Times'* Lex noted last week (December 17), "Russia is redefining the idea of a hard landing. After annual growth averaging 7 per cent for 10 years, the signs are its economy could shrink this quarter and next—the first recession since 1998." As recently as the first half of 2008, the Russian economy was growing at 8 per cent, fuelled by the surge in global prices for oil and other commodities. With the collapse of oil prices after July and global financial markets in September, Russia has been hard hit. Exports have collapsed, industrial production plummeted by nearly 9 per cent in November (y-o-y), the ongoing domestic financial crunch is severe, share prices are down 70 per cent since January, forex reserves have dropped by $150 billion since August despite significant currency depreciation, and refinancing of external borrowings has become very difficult. Goldman Sachs and Barclays Capital project a big decline in investment and hardly any growth in 2009, though some others are a little more optimistic.

Table 7.1

Economic Growth of BRICs (%)

	2007	*2008 (E)*	*2009 (F)*			
			WB	*GS*	*Citi*	*Author*
Brazil	5.4	5.2	2.8	1.5	3.0	2-3
Russia	8.1	6.0	3.0	0.5	4.5	1-2
India	9.0	6.3	5.8	5.8	5.5	4-6
China	11.9	9.4	7.5	6.0	8.2	5-7

Note: E = Estimate; F= Forecast; WB = World Bank; GS = Goldman Sachs. Data for India refer to fiscal year.

Source: World Bank (Global Economic Prospects), Goldman Sachs and Citi (all publications/forecasts are dated December, 2008). Data for 2007 and 2008 from World Bank.

In India too, the damage from global recession is substantial. The growth of the Indian economy had already slowed to 7.5 per cent in the first half of FY 2008/09. Following the global credit crunch of September economic activity decelerated sharply. Merchandise exports fell by 12 per cent in October (y-o-y) and a similar amount in November. Industrial growth turned negative in October for the first time in over 15 years. Sales data across a broad spectrum of Indian industry and services suggest that November would be worse. The rupee has depreciated by 20 per cent in the past few months and forex reserves are down by over $ 60 billion since March. Despite some recent recovery, stock prices are less than half their January peak in rupees and down by more than 60 per cent in dollars. The World Bank, Goldman Sachs and Citi, all expect economic growth in 2009 to be below 6 per cent.

What about the big daddy of the BRICs, the emerging superpower called China? This was the country which had been a major force behind the global growth spurt of 2003-2007 and had largely propelled the massive commodity boom of 2006-2008. There were many who thought that China could be the world's saviour in this crisis. Alas, even the mighty Chinese economy is being severely buffeted by this global tempest. In November, Chinese export growth turned negative after many years. Industrial growth slumped to 5 per cent from the recent trend rates in the mid-teens. Tens of thousands of factories producing toys, textiles, electronics, and other labour-intensive exports closed across the eastern seaboard. The Shanghai stock index is down nearly 70 per cent since the beginning of the year (in dollars). With world trade growth expected to be negligible or negative in 2009 and exports accounting for 40 per cent of China's GDP, the country's economic growth is bound to slow sharply in 2009. Goldman Sachs expects China's growth to drop to 6 per cent, though some others still expect a better outcome.

In the last column of the table I have outlined my own expectations for BRIC growth in 2009, based on the projections presented here as well as others. As Alexandre Marinis has pointed out (*Business Standard*, December 21): if the US, Europe and Japan contract at 2 per cent in 2009, and other non-BRICs show no growth, the BRICs would have to grow by 11 per cent or so to keep world growth out of negative territory. The simple truth is that BRICs are still too small to be global locomotors unless they sustain double digit growth, which they manifestly can't in the present environment. Of course, the fact that the Asian BRICs are still expected to enjoy moderate growth in 2009, is itself testimony to their resilience in the face of global recession. But decoupled they are not.

Where then are the engines to haul the world economy out of stagnation? It does look as if we have to wait for a recovery of the usual suspects: the US, Europe and Japan. And that doesn't seem at all likely in 2009. Let's just hope that a year from now the massive fiscal and monetary stimuli injected (and planned) in these big economies will have done the trick and we will be on the cusp of a global recovery. Or may be we can engineer a turnaround for ourselves?

Business Standard, December 25, 2008.

II

Macroeconomic Policy

8 Exchange Rate Policy

As I have written on many occasions over the past decade, India's post-1991 exchange rate policy has been an important determinant of the country's economic successes since then. Most recently (*Business Standard*, August 22, 2006), I wrote, "Against a background of continuing strong capital inflows...and rising oil prices, RBI (presumably with government support) has prevented undue real appreciation of the rupee, nurtured two-way variation in the exchange rate and moderated excess volatility. This has been no mean feat, especially in view of the concomitant challenge to 'sterilize' the monetary consequences of reserve accretion...The successful management of the exchange rate has been a key determinant of dynamic exports (goods and services) and steadily rising inward remittances." In recent months this cornerstone of India's macroeconomic policy appears to be teetering, as significant appreciation (nominal and real) threatens the dynamism of exports and industrial growth (see, for example, Rajwade, *Business Standard*, April 4 and Ranade, *Business Standard*, April 19).

What is the nature of India's exchange rate policy? What are some of its past successes? Why is the policy now under threat? What should be done? Read on for answers.

After the step devaluations of June 1991 and the phased transition to a "market-determined, unified exchange rate" by March 1993, the RBI (with MoF support) has followed a policy of "managed flexibility" within a system of partial capital account controls. In practice, this has meant fairly active RBI intervention in forex markets to moderate market-driven volatility and maintain a "competitive" exchange rate. The latter has meant using the 1993/94 value of the 6 (earlier 5) currency, trade-weighted, real effective exchange rate (REER) index as a benchmark or informal guidepost (not a formal target).

In the jargon of open economy macroeconomics, this system has clearly been an "intermediate" exchange rate regime, falling between full flexibility (or pure float) and a fixed-rate regime (achieved through monetary union or a currency board). The combination of managed flexibility and partial capital account controls has allowed India to resolve, to a large extent, the trilemma of the famed "Impossible Trinity", which disallows the simultaneous achievement of exchange rate stability, monetary independence and capital market integration (see Figure 8.1). Any two of these goals may be attained (at the vertices of the triangle) but never all three. With the help of partial capital controls India has successfully enjoyed substantial monetary independence and a fair degree of exchange rate flexibility. In practice, it has certainly helped that all three RBI governors of the past 15 years and most finance ministers (and their relevant mandarins) have mastered the nature of the system, and its potentialities and pitfalls.

The economic merits of India's exchange rate system have been demonstrated repeatedly. For example, during the inward foreign capital surge of 1993-1995, despite textbook IMF advice to the contrary, we successfully resisted nominal appreciation of the rupee and built up forex reserves, thus nurturing the nascent export boom of the period and pre-empting increased protectionist resistance to the ongoing programme of customs tariff reductions. Again, during the Asian (and later the Russian) financial crisis of 1997-98, downward (but managed) flexibility of the exchange rate was crucial (together with tight rein on short-term external debt, capital controls on residents and some monetary tightening) in warding off any serious contagion effects. Over the entire period, judicious and flexible management of the exchange rate system has played a critical role in helping India to increase significantly her share in global exports of both goods and services and tripling the ratio of current external receipts to GDP from 8 per cent in 1990/91 to 24 per cent in 2005/06.

If the system has worked so well, what explains the recent oddity of sharp nominal and real appreciation of the rupee, which has seen the six-currency REER index (1993/94=100) rise from 101 in the summer of 2006 to 112 in mid-April 2007 to the consternation of exporters and many others? Frankly, it is both puzzling and distressing. Amongst possible reasons are the following: first, perhaps the recent foreign capital surge (at a time of rising inflation) has overwhelmed the RBI's capacity for "sterilisation" of purchased reserves through the market stabilisation scheme (MSS) and other instruments and thus weakened its willingness to buy forex (since unsterilised forex purchases would augment liquidity and fuel inflation). Second, the finance ministry (and RBI?) may be giving undue weight to a recently fashionable (and simplistic) view that appreciation of the rupee helps contain inflation. Actually, in India, it has modest impact at high cost in terms of industrial competitiveness, exports, growth and employment, especially when India's giant Asian competitor, China, with seven times the value of our exports, follows a sticky exchange rate policy. Third, the recent puzzling rupee appreciation may be just another symptom of weak coordination between RBI and MoF that has been distressingly evident in recent times.

Whatever the reason, it's high time the recent appreciation is reversed and the time-tested policy restored before serious, lasting damage is inflicted on exports, growth and employment. If this requires augmenting RBI's capacity for sterilised intervention through the MSS or other means, so be it. (The quasi-fiscal costs of this policy are well-known, manageable and far outweighed by the benefits of higher exports, growth and employment associated with a lower REER.) If it requires some tightening of constraints on external commercial borrowing by Indian corporates for domestic expenditures (to slow capital surge through this route), so be it. That might also level the playing field a bit in favour of smaller firms in the present context of tighter domestic credit conditions. To those ideologically predisposed to oppose any regulatory restraint, I should point out that successful management of intermediate exchange rate regimes generally involves some compromise with the "market knows best" principle. It's all a matter of balance. If it requires more liberalisation of capital account outflows (consistent with Tarapore II recommendations), that would also help. If it simply needs better coordination of macroeconomic policies between MoF and RBI, surely that's both desirable and possible.

Whatever it takes, it better be done and done soon, if the country is to be spared the avoidable costs of an overvalued exchange rate in terms of foregone growth in exports, output and employment.

Business Standard, April 26, 2007.

Figure 8.1

The Impossible Trinity

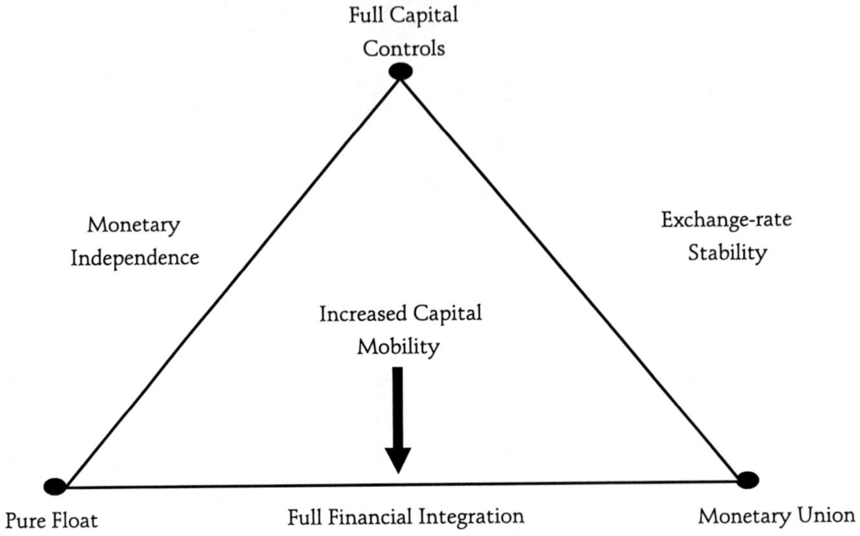

Source: Jeffrey Frankel, "No single currency regime is right for all countries at all times," *Princeton Essays in International Finance* No.215, August 1999.

Table 8.1

6-Currency REER Index of Rupee (1993/94 = 100)

1993/94		100.0
1996/97		101.0
1999/2000		97.5
2002/03		97.4
2005/06		106.7
2006/07		
	Jun.	101.8
	Jul.	101.3
	Aug.	101.2
	Sept.	103.9
	Oct.	106.5
	Nov.	107.1
	Dec.	106.0
	Jan.	108.2
	Feb.	108.6
	Mar.	108.4
	Apr. 18.	112.2

Source: RBI, *Macroeconomic and Monetary Developments, Fourth Quarter Review 2006-07* (April 2007), and *RBI Monthly Bulletin*, April 2007.

9 Midsummer Madness?

The Greeks said, "Those the gods wish to destroy, they first make mad." The aphorism comes to mind when assessing the UPA government's recent policies towards external capital inflows and exchange rate management. As everyone knows, the ministry of finance (MoF) and RBI have been confronted by the challenge of surging capital inflows over the past five years. Until early 2007, the RBI had managed to insulate its hugely successful exchange rate policy from these surging capital inflows (see my piece in *Business Standard* of April 26, 2007). But then things seemed to fall apart as the Rs/$ rate appreciated from around 44 to 40 and there were corresponding changes in various real effective exchange rate indices. The predicted costs of this avoidable rupee appreciation are now showing up in the economic data and include marked slowdown in exports of goods and services, sudden pressure from cheap imports on import-substituting activities, rising job losses in labour-using industries like textiles, sharply mounting trade deficits, and massive problems of liquidity management. There is more to come.

Reams have been written on this subject in all the pink papers, some of it sensible, quite a lot of it not. I will not rehearse the well-worn arguments. Instead let me focus on what I see as the two main proximate causes of this major policy failure and suggest solutions. First is the hugely counter-productive policy of MoF to enhance the annual external commercial borrowing (ECB) limit for domestic borrowers in each of the last two fiscal years, thus aggravating enormously the underlying problem of managing the surge in external capital inflows. Just how serious this policy error has been can be gauged from the recent BoP data in Table 9.1. In round numbers, while the current account deficit stayed almost constant between 2005/06 and 2006/07, the capital account surplus increased by $22 billion, of which ECB accounted for over $13 billion, or 60 per cent of the increase. To prevent unwanted rupee appreciation, the RBI had to purchase the extra $22 billion into reserves in 2006/07, compounding massively its liquidity management challenges. The $13 billion of additional ECB corresponds to over Rs. 55,000 crores of reserve money injection (at prevailing exchange rates). To put that into perspective, a 0.5 per cent CRR increase only "sterilises" about Rs. 15,000 crores.

Table 9.1

India's Summary Balance of Payments (US $billion)

	2005/06	2006/07	Change
Current Account (net)	**- 9.2**	**- 9.6**	**- 0.4**
Capital Account (net)	**24.2**	**46.2**	**+ 22.0**
of which:			
Foreign Direct Investment	4.7	8.4	+ 3.7
Portfolio Investment	12.5	7.1	- 5.4
External Commercial Borrowing	2.7[1]	16.1	+ 13.4
Short-term Trade Credit	1.7	3.3	+ 1.6
External Assistance	1.7	1.8	+ 0.1
NRI Deposits	2.8	3.9	+ 1.1
Addition to Reserves[2]	**15.1**	**36.6**	**+21.5**

Note: 1. Net of IMD redemptions of $5.5 billion.
2. Balance of payments basis (excluding valuation changes).

Source: RBI's "Macroeconomic and Monetary Developments, First Quarter, 2007/8", July 2007.

Against this background, several analysts (aside from myself) have called for a reversal of ECB policy to moderate the (self-inflicted?) capital surge problem. Of these, Rajeev Malik of J.P. Morgan (not usually identified as a fount of socialist control policies) has been the most trenchant advocate in a series of articles in this journal since spring of this year. More recently, the PM's Economic Advisory Council has lent its considerable weight to this view. All of us are careful to avoid any significant negative "signaling effect" on foreign investment, either direct or portfolio. Temporarily constraining domestic borrowers' access to ECB is a limitation, but seems well worth the benefits of containing capital surge and allowing a more competitive exchange rate policy, without spawning excess liquidity or unduly high fiscal costs from sterilised intervention. Any qualms should be assuaged by the interesting fact that some 20 or so corporates have accounted for over half of all ECB borrowings in recent years (Table 9.2 lists top 10 borrowers in 2006/07; they accounted for over 30 per cent of total approvals). Needless to say, these corporates have done rather well financially from the recent rupee appreciation and will deploy their considerable clout in resisting any reversal (a clout magnified by approaching elections?).

Table 9.2

Top 10 ECB Borrowers for the Year 2006/07 (by Approvals/Registration)

S.No.	Company	ECBs/FCCBs (in $ million)	Share (%)
1	Reliance Petroleum Ltd.	2,000	7.89
2	Reliance Communications Ltd.	1,000	3.94
3	Tata Steel Ltd.	755	2.98
4	Reliance Industries Ltd.	750	2.96
5	Reliance Energy Limited	650	2.56
6	Air India Ltd.	560	2.21
7	Export-Import Bank of India	550	2.17
8	Reliance Ports and Terminals Ltd.	500	1.97
9	Reliance Communications Infrastructure Ltd.	500	1.97
10	Reliance Telecom Ltd.	500	1.97
	Sub-total	**7,765**	**30.62**
	Total for year	**25,353**	**100.00**

Source: www.rbi.org.in/scripts/ECBView/aspx

The second principal proximate cause of the recent rupee appreciation appears to be the "conversion" of MoF (and RBI?) to a pro-appreciation set of arguments peddled in recent months by some IMF staffers and a small group of younger domestic economists. A common characteristic of both these sets of bright, well-trained economists is a notable lack of hands-on, policy-making experience in a world of real political economy constraints and real uncertainties. Incidentally, during the previous episode of capital surge in 1993-1995, IMF staffers had proffered the same recommendation of rupee appreciation (in those days they didn't publish in our pink papers!). Despite having just emerged from an IMF loan programme, we (in MoF) listened politely and ignored the advice, thus protecting the emerging booms in exports and industry. Alas, the present MoF appears to have been more receptive to the pro-appreciation nostrums. Perhaps this is because these arguments are anchored in textbook views of open economy macro policy, which have deeply (and perhaps appropriately) influenced policies in advanced industrial nations. The textbooks are fine; it's just that their domain of greatest relevance is restricted to $20,000 (plus) per capita, mature industrial economies with well-developed financial markets and "deep integration" of domestic and external markets in goods and services. The textbook policy recommendations have to be carefully screened and calibrated to our rapidly transforming, $1000 per capita economy, with massive rural underemployment, semi-developed financial institutions and markets, bad physical and social infrastructure, and substantial labour market dualism.

Let me illustrate with a few "textbook propositions" (favoured by the pro-appreciation folk) and my comments on them:

Proposition1: Central banks (notably RBI) should focus on the single objective of inflation control.

Comment: Wrong. At our stage of development, the RBI is quite right to weigh and pursue several objectives, including inflation, economic activity, financial stability and institutional development.

Proposition 2: The RBI should not concern itself with the level or volatility of the exchange rate.

Comment: Nonsense. The exchange rate is the single most important price in the economic domain, which deeply influences the rate of economic development, the degree of openness and the balance between tradables and non-tradables. It would be criminal for the RBI (and MoF) not to have clear strategic goals and instruments for exchange rate management, within the limits set by its objectives and the external payments system.

Proposition 3: Inflation is a purely monetary phenomenon; so monetary policy is all that really matters.

Comment: Wrong again, at least if you examine carefully the empirical evidence in developing economies. Supply shocks, market rigidities, expectations and openness, all matter rather a lot.

Proposition 4: As productivity increases in the economy the appropriate exchange rate should appreciate commensurately.

Comment: Not quite. Yes, productivity growth is an important variable in calibrating exchange rate policy but a lot depends on what's happening in key competitor countries (China and others).

Proposition 5: Sterilised intervention (purchase of dollars by the RBI, offset by sale of rupee securities) always leads to higher interest rates.

Comment: Rubbish. It is quite feasible to calibrate the intervention so as to leave interest rate and liquidity conditions roughly where they were before the specified dollar purchase-cum-sterilisation.

I could go on, but you get the picture.

To sum up, our exchange rate policy since March 2007 has erred seriously and imposed significant, rising and avoidable costs for exports, output and employment. Given my view of the proximate causes, the solutions are clear enough: sharply tighten the present ECB policy and get real about macroeconomic policy in the real world. At this juncture, global uncertainties may also help correct our faulty exchange rate policies.

Postscript: This article was submitted just before the government's announcement of tightening ECB norms. This policy correction is welcome; let's hope it's enough.

Business Standard, August 9, 2007.

10 Too Little, Too Late?

Some six months ago (*Business Standard*, 26 April 2007), I criticised "the authorities" (MinFin and RBI) for the abrupt shift in India's exchange rate policy in March 2007, which entailed a fairly sharp appreciation of the rupee. It's time to revisit the issue and assess developments over the past six months. But before doing so, let me reiterate a couple of key points made in my April piece, which seems to have eluded some participants in the debate.

First, the sharp horns of the trilemma posed by the textbook *Impossible Trinity* (simultaneous attainment of exchange rate stability, monetary independence, and capital account convertibility) are substantially blunted for India by the presence of partial capital controls. This allows us to retain significant autonomy over both monetary policy and exchange rate management. It is tiresome to have the trilemma argument trotted out repeatedly by commentators who should know better. Second, contrary to popular belief, the substantial appreciation of the rupee in recent times (see Figure 10.1) is not just a problem for exporters. It's also a problem for all other domestic producers of tradable goods and services, who face cheaper import competition. More broadly, the available evidence indicates that exchange rate appreciation poses a significant threat to growth of output and employment (see Surjit Bhalla, *Business Standard*, August 18, 2007).

Turning to post-April developments, there is both good news and bad news. Leading with the latter, there has been a predictable slowdown in export growth of goods and services, with rupee earnings stagnant or even negative in some labour-intensive sub-sectors such as textiles and leather products. While the foreign trade data do not show this, there is increasing reportage in the pink papers of labour-intensive manufacturers for the domestic market struggling to survive, retrenching or even closing in the face of cheaper import competition. Given the usual lags between orders and sales, these adverse costs of rupee appreciation are likely to mount.

Figure 10.1

Exchange Rate

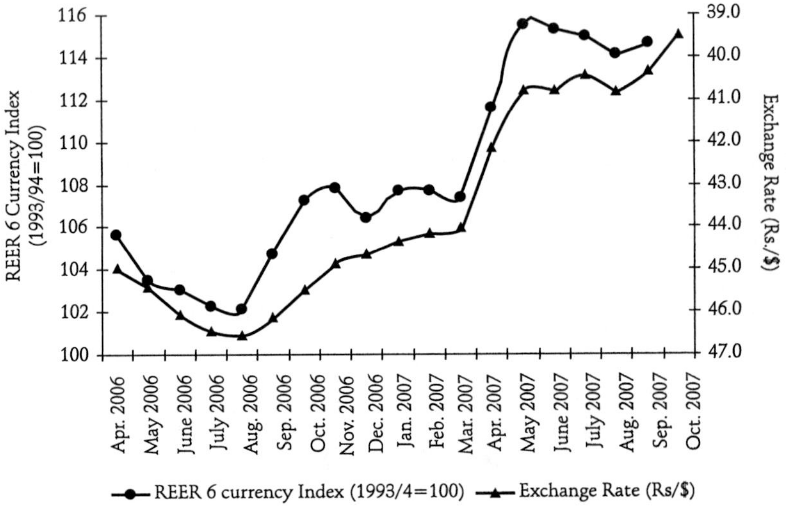

Source: http://www.rbi.org.in/scripts/Statistics.aspx, http://www.fedai.org.in/WeeklyAverageRates.xls

On the positive side, the backlash to the pre-May rupee appreciation seems to have elicited some desirable corrections in official policy along the lines recommended in my April article (no causation claimed!). The RBI's tools for countering the continuing surge in foreign capital inflow, which is the underlying pressure for appreciation, have been strengthened by augmenting the size of Market Stabilisation Scheme (MSS). The RBI has used this instrument (together with CRR increases and LAF operations) to bolster its purchases of the incoming foreign exchange and "sterilise" their liquidity consequences. Thus, forex reserves rose by a hefty $62 billion between 1st April and late October this year. Second, the MinFin moved, at last, in early August to reverse its earlier policy error of premature (and untimely) liberalisation of external commercial borrowing (ECB) policy, which led to the massive surge in ECB net inflows to over $16 billion in 2006/07, followed by another $7 billion in the first quarter of the current year (for more on this, see my piece in *Business Standard*, August 9, 2007). Last fortnight, SEBI has acted, under MinFin guidance, to tighten the guidelines for participatory notes (P-notes) and other offshore derivatives on Indian shares. In this context, the finance minister has clearly acknowledged on television the need to "moderate foreign capital inflows" and has opined that the currently elevated rupee exchange rate was above the government's "comfort zone".

As a result of all this, especially the RBI's dogged and sustained intervention in the forex market, the six-currency real effective exchange rate (REER) index of the rupee has stabilised around 115 (1993/94=100 base) since May and even the bilateral Rs/$ rate has not appreciated significantly beyond the 40.8 level of May 2007 (see Figure 10.1). And this has been accomplished despite the recent upswing in capital inflows (especially FII investments) after the US Fed's loosening of monetary policy in September and the ensuing surge of equity flows to premium emerging markets.

Good as they may seem, these results are far from adequate. A REER index level 11-12 per cent higher than in summer 2006 is much above the "comfort zone" for healthy and sustained growth of tradable goods and services and employment in them. And the struggle to hold the line seems to be getting harder. As several analysts have noted, surging foreign capital inflows and rising forex reserves are not an uniquely Indian phenomenon. China and a number of other emerging market countries have confronted similar challenges. Yet, their exchange rate appreciation over the past year is typically less than the rupee's. This begs the obvious question about the effectiveness of India's policies in this domain. Has it all been a case of too little too late? Certainly that's the impression one gets when it comes to "moderating" ECB and FII inflows.

So what is to be done? First, the MSS limits need to be swiftly augmented to empower the RBI to move much more aggressively to purchase forex and sterilise the counterpart rupees. The goal should be to bring down the REER index to the order of 110, preferably lower. Second, the belated steps taken by MinFin on August 7 to tighten ECB policy should be implemented faithfully, without too many special "exceptions". Third, the recent tightening of guidelines on P-notes may need to be revisited with a view to mandating swifter unwinding of P-notes. Fourth, the grant of ad hoc fiscal "sops" to exporters to compensate them for rupee appreciation should be discontinued. Aside from being arbitrary, untidy and fiscally unsound, such sops only compensate a sub-set of the producers hurt by appreciation. More importantly, they distract from the correct policy, which is to reverse much of the recent appreciation. Fifth, there should be a systematic and coordinated (between MinFin and RBI) review of available options to deal with the special challenges posed by the unprecedented surge in foreign capital inflows into the country.

If all this sounds too heterodox and "market unfriendly", then buckle up for the turbulence on the alternative "market knows best" trajectory: the rupee continues to appreciate to 35/$ (or 30?) within a year; exports and import-competing activities become increasingly uncompetitive; the trade deficit widens further to well above the seven per cent of GDP of 2006/07 and service exports nosedive; retrenchments proliferate and unemployment increases; economic growth flags; foreign investors lose confidence, take fright and seek to exit; the exchange rate plummets; and we are back to Rs. 50/$ (or 60?) after having laid waste to large swathes of the productive economy, not to mention bankrupting the financial system. Sounds unlikely? Don't be too sure. Stupid policies can beget some pretty bad outcomes. That's the lesson of economic history, including our own. Oh yes, and there may be some political consequences as well.

Business Standard, November 8, 2007.

11 RBI Should Cut Rates Now!

As most readers know, I have been a staunch supporter of the RBI's modulated management of monetary policy over the last few years. (I was also an admirer of RBI's deft exchange rate management until it succumbed to misguided government pressure and allowed the infamous and sharp rupee appreciation of spring 2007... but that's another story, which I have told in previous columns.) In the past few months I find myself at odds with RBI's monetary policy. In a nutshell, I believe the RBI has fallen behind the curve in taking timely, anticipatory action to reduce policy interest rates. Specifically, the downswing in policy rates should have begun in October. Since that opportunity was ignored (as well as the one in January), the case for a sharper cut, in the order of 50-75 basis points in the repo rate, is now strong and should be acted on immediately. Let me elaborate.

The case for a swift and sizeable reduction in the repo rate rests on several pillars. First, and most importantly, there is mounting evidence that the five-year old surge in India's economic growth, especially industrial growth, peaked a few months back. Figures 11.1A and 11.1B suggest that industrial growth may have peaked as far back as the final quarter of 2006/07, while GDP growth peaked in the following quarter. In 2007/08, Q2 the annual rate of industrial value added growth dropped below 10 per cent for the first time in seven quarters. More disconcerting is the steeper decline in the 3-month moving average of growth in the industrial production, down to 8 per cent in October 2007 from the above 12 per cent heights it held for several months. Add to this the policy-engineered slackening of bank credit growth to around 20 per cent from 30 per cent a year ago plus the deceleration of headline WPI inflation to below 4 per cent since August 2007 and we have a pretty convincing picture of a slowing industrial economy with low inflation.

Second, a key feature of monetary policy is that it has to be anticipatory, especially given the long and uncertain lags in its impact. Indeed, the recent success of the RBI's monetary policy in balancing exceptionally high economic growth with modest inflation owes a lot to timely and incremental ratcheting up of monetary measures over the past three years. Looking ahead over the coming 12-18 months, it seems clear that global growth will slow significantly because of the subprime-led international credit crunch and high oil prices. So, even though India's GDP growth in 2007/08 notched up a robust 8.7 per cent, the chances of encountering strong headwinds from the international economy are high, not to mention the toll extracted by an overly appreciated rupee. Added to the already apparent slowing of industrial expansion, it seems reasonable to anticipate slowing of GDP growth to below 8 per cent in 2008/09, especially if the current high policy interest rates are retained for a few more months.

Figure 11.1A

Growth of Industry (Value Added) and GDP (year on year)

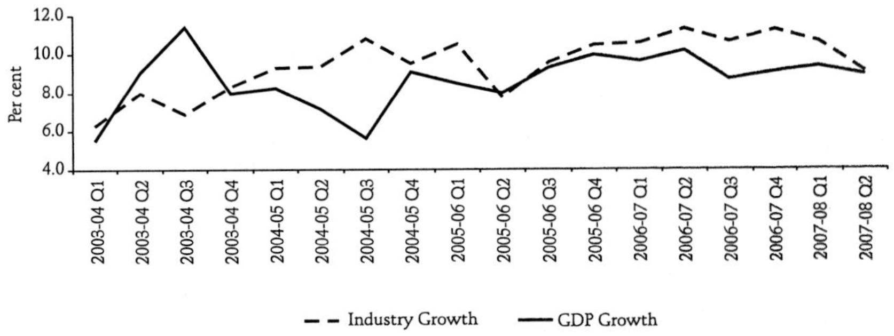

Source: http://mospi.nic.in/mospi_press_releases.htm. Industry = Manufacturing, Mining and Quarrying, Public Utilities and Construction.

Figure 11.1B

Growth of Industrial Production (IIP), year on year

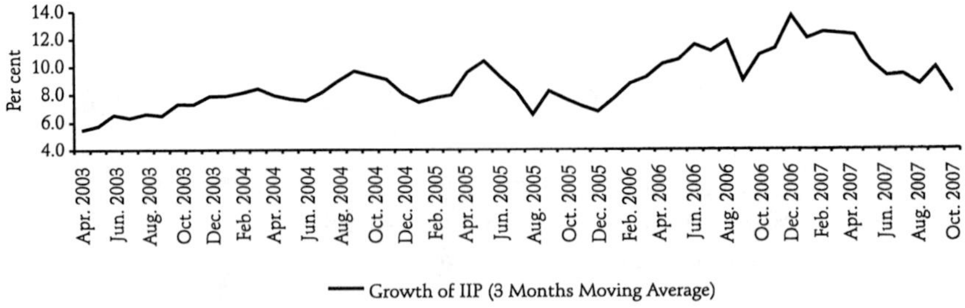

Source: *http://mospi.nic.in/mospi_iip.htm*

Third, as Figure 11.2 shows, the retention of high policy rates in India, when the US Fed Funds rate has been cut aggressively in the past six months, has led to a sharp widening of interest rate differentials with respect to dollar instruments, thus increasing greatly the incentives for higher short-term foreign capital inflows into India and thereby aggravating the key macro policy problem of excess foreign capital surge. In his otherwise misguided piece last week (*Business Standard*, February 6, 2008) Ajay Shah also emphasises this valid point, though he fails to mention the central role of bad government policy (over the past three years) in undermining partial capital controls on external commercial borrowing and dodgy portfolio inflows. It is this policy weakness which perhaps provoked an anguished plea from the RBI Governor in his monetary policy statement a fortnight back: "…it is critical for public policy to effectively, demonstrably and convincingly indicate the commitment to managing capital flows consistent with macro fundamentals through appropriate and decisive policy actions."

Figure 11.2

RBI Policy Rates vs US Fed Funds Rate

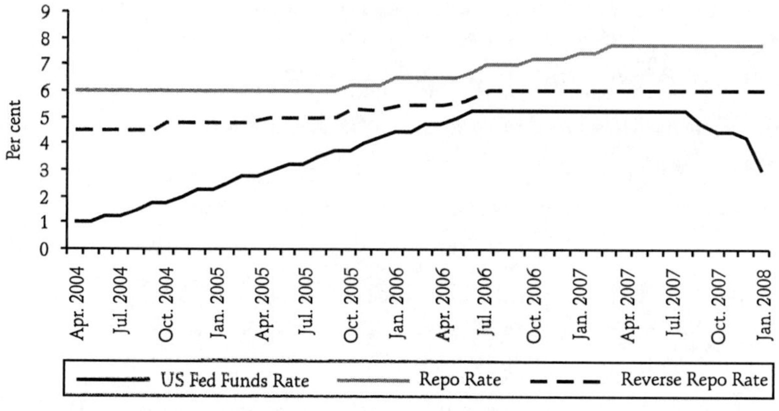

Source: *http://www.rbi.org.in/scripts/BS_ViewBulletin.aspx?Id=8852*
http://www.newyorkfed.org/markets/statistics/dlyrates/fedrate.html

Fourth, India is perhaps unique in maintaining such a wide band of 175 basis points between the repo and reverse repo rates in the money market. The economic basis for this is dubious. For quite a long period, between April 2005 and September 2006 this band was a much more acceptable 100 basis points. A reduction of 50-75 basis points would help reduce the present unduly large gap.

Finally (and here my argument is more tentative), the recent, sharp correction and subsequent volatility in equity markets could take a disproportionate toll of "animal spirits" propelling real investment growth.

A prompt reduction in policy rates (undertaken for the more traditional four reasons outlined above) could have a mitigating influence.

Let me now deal briefly with some arguments against a reduction in policy rates.

Argument 1: Available data still point to strong investment growth. So why cut rates?

Counter: True. But investment slowdowns can be sudden and painful. In any case, given monetary policy lags, waiting for clearer signals of slackening investment could make the rate reductions tardy.

Argument 2: Inflationary pressures still persist, especially from energy and agriculture. So the policy rates should remain high.

Counter: Yes, the inflationary potential of commodity shortages persists. But aggregate inflation is well within RBI's stated comfort zone. Moreover, such supply-side price pressures suggest less responsiveness to monetary measures. Put differently, the growth-inflation trade-off is steeper for inelastic-supply-driven price rises. I would maintain that the risks to growth are now higher than of inflation.

Argument 3: A rate cut now might reflate the bubbles in equity and real estate prices leading to more pain down the road.

Counter: Perhaps. But this risk is low. Most commentators believe that market participants have internalised the salutary lessons of recent turbulence.

Argument 4: There is plenty of liquidity still sloshing around. Look at the size of the "liquidity overhang". Any way, who is stopping the banks from reducing their deposit and lending rates?

Counter: First, the so-called "liquidity overhang" is more a measure of RBI's intervention to sterilise excess capital inflows. The correct solution to the problem is not to maintain high policy rates but for the government to respond effectively to RBI's plea for more effective capital account management. As for banks and other intermediaries autonomously reducing rates, surely the RBI should lead with policy rate signals. Have we forgotten the potency of central bank policy rate signals?

So, with apologies to Lewis Carroll, "The time has come," the Walrus said, "the time to cut the repo rate is now!"

Business Standard, February 14, 2008.

12 The Savings-Investment Miracle

Many factors contribute to economic growth of a country. Most economists would agree that one key determinant is aggregate investment. (Remember the famous Harrod-Domar growth model of the 1940s?) The faster the capital stock of a country increases the more rapid will be its rate of growth of national output. And investment, of course, depends crucially on the level of savings in the economy. India's remarkable growth of the last five years, at around 8.5 per cent a year, certainly supports this view. Both savings and investment have recorded extraordinary buoyancy in this period. It's a largely untold story. So let's spend a little time on the basic numbers.

Table 12.1 presents two-year averages of savings and investment (as a percentage of GDP) at five-year intervals over the past two decades. A brief inspection of the table brings out the following highlights. First, the total investment rate hardly changed between the early 1990s and the first years of the current decade, holding steady at about 24 per cent of GDP. In the next five years it surged dramatically to about 36 per cent in 2005-2007 (according to the government's "Advance Estimates" the level rose further to 38.4 per cent in 2007/08). Second, this unprecedented increase in aggregate investment by 12 per cent of GDP in five years was matched by an almost equal spurt in domestic savings from 23.6 per cent of GDP in 2000-2002 to 34.5 per cent in 2005-2007. Third, India has had very little recourse to net foreign savings (equivalent to the current account deficit on the balance of payments) throughout the entire period, especially in the present decade.

What explains this truly exceptional boom in aggregate savings and investment in India? To get a proper understanding, we need a good deal of serious research on this phenomenon. Till the scholars do their stuff, let me offer some preliminary thoughts. Let's approach the matter from the savings side and look at the components (see Table 12.1 and Figure 12.1). The most important component of domestic savings in India is households (including unincorporated enterprises). The ratio of household savings rose fairly steadily from about 13 per cent of GDP in 1985-1987 to 22 per cent in 2000-2002, when it accounted for 93 per cent of total savings. This steady increase may

Table 12.1

Savings and Investment (as per cent of GDP at current market prices)

Year (Avg.)	*1985-1987*	*1990-1992*	*1995-1997*	*2000-2002*	*2005-2007*
1. Household Savings	13.2	17.1	16.4	21.9	24.0
2. Private Corporate Savings	1.8	2.9	4.7	3.6	7.6
3. Public Savings	3.7	2.2	2.4	-1.9	2.9
Govt. Administration	(0.5)	(-1.5)	(-1.6)	(-5.8)	(-1.6)
Public Enterprises	(3.2)	(3.7)	(4.0)	(3.9)	(4.5)
4. Gross Domestic Savings	**18.7**	**22.2**	**23.6**	**23.6**	**34.5**
5. Net Foreign Savings	2.1	1.9	1.5	0.0	1.2
6. Gross Domestic Investment	**20.8**	**24.0**	**25.1**	**23.6**	**35.7**

Source: CSO (*http://mospi.nic.in/mospi_cso_rept_pubn.htm*)

Figure 12.1

Savings as per cent of GDP at Current Market Prices
(3 Year Rolling Average)

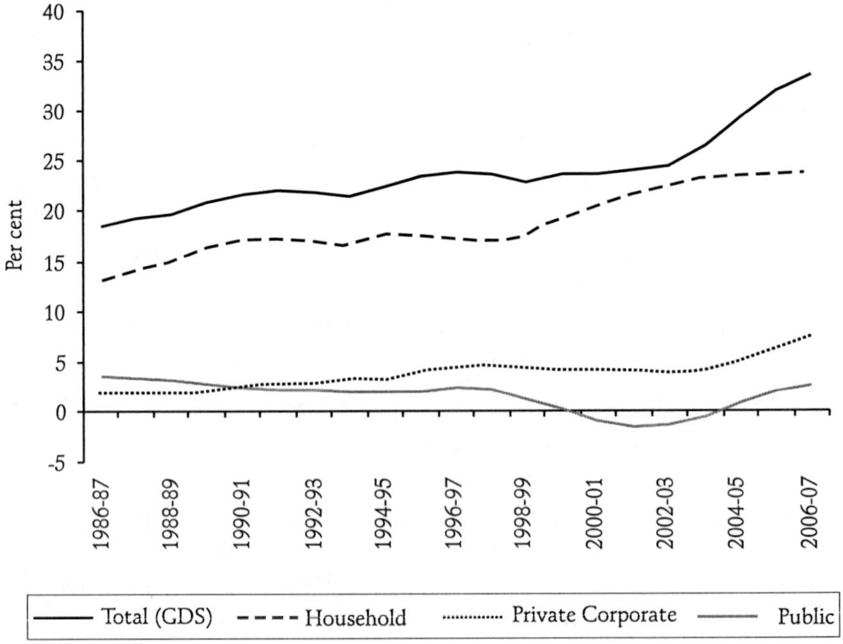

Source: http://mospi.nic.in/mospi_cso_rept_pubn.htm

be attributed to several factors, including rising average incomes and the demographic dividend of a growing share of the population in the working age group. Yet, somewhat surprisingly, household savings contributed only an additional 2 per cent of GDP over the most recent five years. The remainder of the 11 per cent (of GDP) increase in total savings came from private companies and the public sector (government and enterprises).

Private corporate savings (consisting of depreciation provisions and retained earnings) more than doubled from 3.6 per cent of GDP in 2000-2002 to 7.6 per cent in 2005-2007 (in 2007/08 it may exceed 8 per cent). This is an astounding increase, especially in view of the fact that this ratio never exceeded 5 per cent of GDP in any year prior to 2004/05. It is, of course, consistent with the extraordinary growth in corporate earnings that has been witnessed in recent years. Even more impressive has been the surge in corporate investment from under 6 per cent of GDP in 2000-2002 to nearly 14 per cent in 2005-2007 (see also Figure 12.2). By 2006/07 private companies accounted for over 40 per cent of total investment, exceeding the peak share attained in the mid-1990s investment boom. Indeed, it is very likely that surging corporate investment was a powerful driver of much higher corporate savings. Either way, this exceptional episode should keep the seekers of causation busy for a long time.

Figure 12.2

Gross Domestic Capital Formation as Per cent of GDP at Current Market Prices (3 Year Rolling Average)

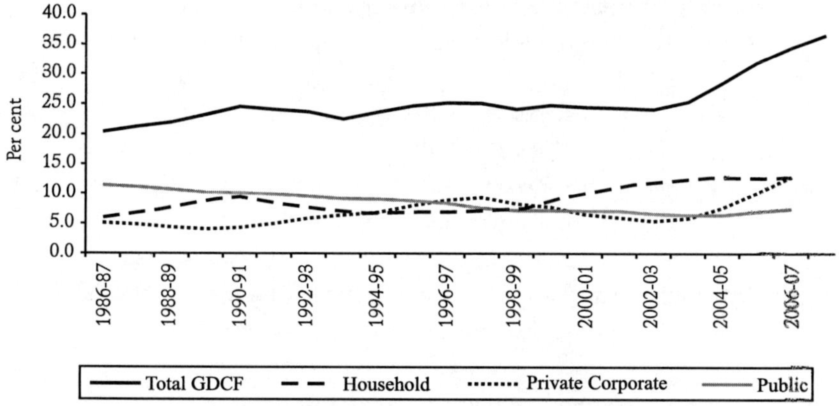

Note: GDCF is adjusted for errors and omissions.

Source: *http://mospi.nic.in/mospi_cso_rept_pubn.htm*
http://mospi.nic.in/mospi_press_releases.htm

The biggest contributor to the savings explosion after 2001/02 has been the public sector. Public savings went from minus 1.9 per cent of GDP in 2000-2002 to plus 2.9 per cent in 2005-2007, a massive turnaround of nearly 5 per cent of GDP. As the Table 12.1 shows, the bulk of this improvement occurred in "government" (at all levels), with only a modest increase in the enterprise sub-sector. Among the factors responsible for this very welcome improvement in government savings were: the central fiscal responsibility law passed by the Parliament in 2003; the proliferation of similar laws in state governments, triggered largely by the debt relief inducements recommended by the Twelfth Finance Commission; the buoyancy of state tax revenues resulting from the switch-over to VAT; and the tremendous increase in Central direct tax revenues spurred by the massive growth of corporate earnings and fast-growing pay packets among the urban salariat.

To put it simply (and eliding over the complexities of a richer causal story), India's aggregate investment rose by an unprecedented 12 per cent of GDP after 2001/02 because of an 11 per cent increase in domestic savings, which came from the public sector (5 per cent), private companies (4 per cent) and households (2 per cent). And all these numbers might look even more impressive after official data for 2007/08 become available.

The big question today is will this massive surge in savings and investment ratios continue into 2008/09 and beyond? The chances are that it won't and here's why. The household savings ratio will probably continue to increase gradually for much the same reasons that have prevailed over the last two decades, except that in 2008/09 we might see some moderation due to negative wealth effects stemming from lower asset prices (equity and real estate). The corporate savings boom is more likely to peter out as the industrial economy continues to slow in the face of global headwinds from the international credit crunch, domestic business cycles and high interest rates. Depending, obviously, on earnings performance, the ratio of corporate savings to GDP could easily drop below eight per cent. Central government savings will be impacted by the Sixth Pay Commission, the budget's income tax bonanza, slower growth in company taxes, farm loan waiver costs and rising major subsidies. Public enterprise savings will bear the brunt of growing oil sector "under-recoveries". On balance, public savings is likely to dip below three per cent of GDP. Taken together, aggregate savings in 2008/09 may be in the range of 34-35 per cent of GDP, compared to the 36-37 per cent peak probably achieved in 2007/08. So aggregate investment could also drop one or two percentage points from the 2007/08 advance estimate of 38.4 per cent of GDP.

In a nutshell, we are more likely to see a leveling off (or even a small decline) in the record levels of aggregate savings and investment attained by the Indian economy, rather than a continuation of further increases. Of course, we won't know for another two years when the official data for 2008/09 savings-investment estimates become public!

Business Standard, March 27, 2008.

III

Economic Growth

13 If Growth were Slower...?

For the past five years or so I have been questioning the credibility and sustainability of the surge in India's services sector since the mid-1990s, as reported in the official national accounts data (see, for example, *Business Standard*, December 23, 2003). A recent joint paper by two Brookings Institution scholars (Bosworth and Collins) and a Planning Commission adviser (Virmani) has catalysed my returning to this subject. Before turning to this paper (by BCV), let me reiterate my major concerns and embellish them graphically.

First, as Figure 13.1 shows, the rate of services sector growth has accelerated noticeably after 1996/97, averaging 8.5 per cent a year in these most recent nine years, compared to an average growth rate of under 6 per cent in the previous three decades. Second, and perhaps even more remarkably, the trajectory of services parted company from that of industry (including construction) after 1996/97. In a one-day cricket parlance, the services "snake" in Figure 13.1, which had till then hugged the industry "snake", surges up and away after 1996/97. Until then the growth of these two sectors tended to be quite closely correlated (Figures 13.1 and 13.2), except in a couple of years of industrial recession when the growth in industry slumped much more steeply than did the growth of services. After 1996/97 (and especially during the Ninth Plan period of 1997-2002) the growth of these two sectors diverged markedly. Services retained its buoyancy despite a fairly prolonged period of slow industrial growth. On average, services grew by 8.5 per cent and industry by only 6 per cent between 1996/97 and 2005/06. (The divergence would be greater if the "construction" sub-sector were grouped with services.)

These divergent trajectories had at least two significant consequences: the share of services in GDP rose quickly to 54 per cent by 2005/06 (compared to 41 per cent in 1990/91 and 50 per cent in 2000/01); and India's services sector accounted for a remarkable (and unprecedented) 67 per cent of all the economic growth recorded between 1996/97 and 2005/06. Nor can this exceptionally high growth contribution of the services sector be explained

Figure 13.1

Gross Domestic Product (Constant 1993/94 Prices) with 1970-71 as Base Year (1970-71=100)

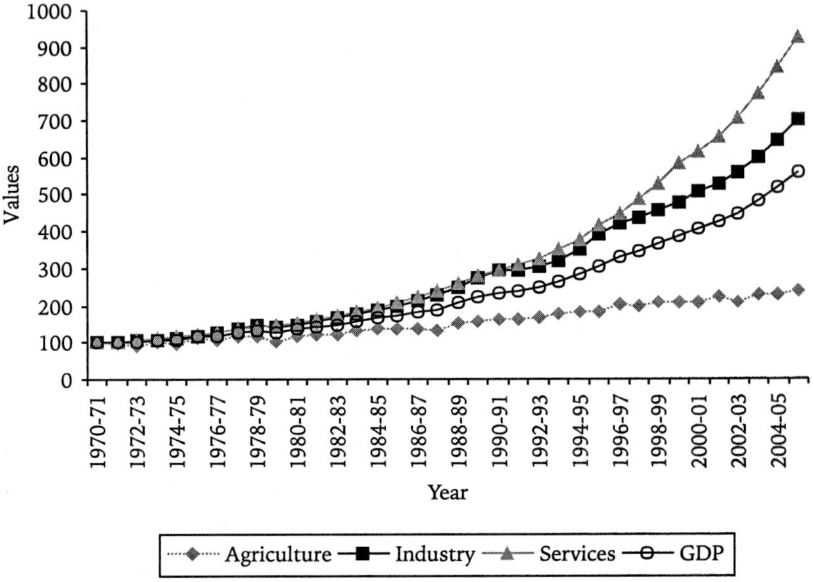

Figure 13.2

Sectoral Growth Rates

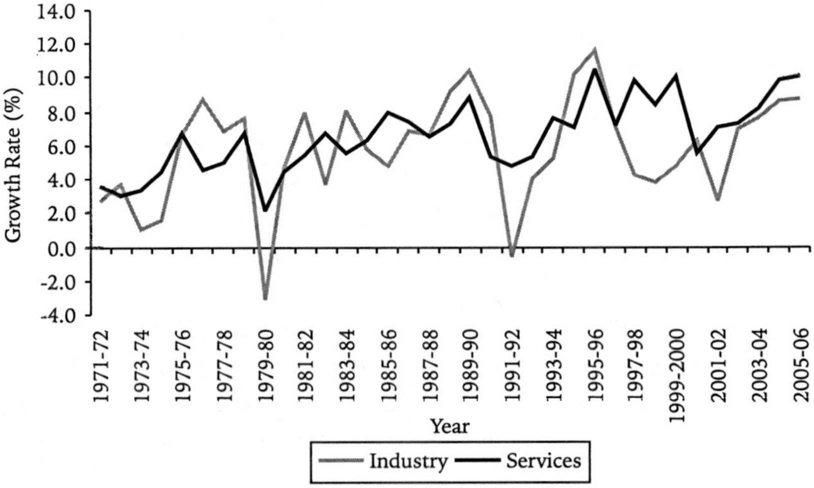

adequately by the indubitably rapid growth of the "modern" segments such as IT, ITES, telecom, and finance. These certainly grew fast but from low bases. Even more important (if less explicable) was the strong growth of "traditional" segments such as wholesale and retail trade (though Walmart had yet to come!), transport, and community and personal services, which account for the preponderant share of India's services sector.

Elsewhere, I have also pointed out that the post-1996/97 pattern of services growing significantly faster than industry is one which finds little resonance in the growth experience of other developing countries. Specifically, in the 35 years, 1965-1999, not one of the seven fastest growing countries (India does not figure in the shortlist) demonstrated faster growth of services over industry. India's post-1996/97 growth pattern really is quite peculiar and puzzling.

In their paper on the "Sources of Growth in the Indian Economy" (presented at a NCAER-Brookings conference in Delhi a few months ago), BCV are similarly perplexed by the high rates of growth of output and productivity they find in the services sector from the mid-1990s onwards. They point out that high rates of productivity growth in "traditional" segments of the services sector are neither expected nor found elsewhere in the world. They go on to speculate that price trends in services may have been underestimated in the official Indian data, leading to overestimation of real growth.

How is one to deal with this situation? Obviously, attempting serious alternative estimates of the country's national income estimates is way beyond the capacity of individuals or even think tanks. Ideally, the CSO should publish a serious discussion paper on the sources and methods of value added estimates in the services sector, which marshals the evidence in support of these estimates and allays the kinds of concerns expressed here. That is what I had hoped for when I wrote three years ago "the methodology of service sector estimates changed significantly in the mid-90s at the time of the transition to the new base year, 1993/94. There is need for serious enquiry to reject the hypothesis that this change in methods may have imparted systematic upward bias to Gross Value Added estimates in key service sectors" (*Business Standard*, December 23, 2003).

In the meantime, let me indulge in a small thought experiment. Let's assume that the official estimates of growth in agriculture and industry are accurate. Let's further assume that after 1996/97, the services sector has grown not at the officially recorded rate but at a rate one per cent higher than whatever is the recorded growth rate for industry in a given year. This assumption (and it is no more than that) draws support from the earlier history of close correlation between the growth of services and industry, and also allows for the indubitable dynamism of some "modern" segments of services such as IT and telecom over the past decade. Based on this assumption we can recompute a fresh trajectory for the growth of GDP (hypothetical).

Table 13.1 gives a comparison between this crudely constructed hypothetical series for GDP growth after 1996/97 and the official series. A couple of points are noteworthy. First, average GDP growth in the past nine years in this hypothetical series is 5.3 per cent, instead of 6.2 per cent as shown by the official series. Second, in the last three years of high growth, the average "hypothetical" GDP growth of 7.5 per cent is reassuringly high and only a little below the officially estimated average of 8.1 per cent (This is because industrial growth in these years was high; so the "correction" implicit in the hypothetical series for services is small). As expected, the main divergence between the official and hypothetical growth series occurs during the Ninth Plan period.

Thought experiments are all very well but what do I really believe? Well... on a balance of considerations (as they are fond of saying in government), I think the hypothetical series for GDP growth in the past nine years may be a little closer to reality than the official series. Other than the arguments offered

Table 13.1

GDP Growth (% per year)

	Official	*Hypothetical**
1997/98	4.8	2.8
1998/99	6.5	4.9
1999/2000	6.1	4.0
2000/01	4.4	5.2
2001/02	5.8	4.7
2002/03	3.8	3.6
2003/04	8.5	7.8
2004/05	7.5	6.6
2005/06	8.4	8.1
1997/98-2005/06 Average	6.2	5.3

Note: * Assumes services sector growth was 1 per cent higher than official industry sector growth.

here I can advance no "proof" for this. It's certainly not a "slam-dunk" case. But I hope it encourages (provokes?) the official national income estimators to make public a well-reasoned case for their estimates of the level and growth in services value added and thus dispel the heretical doubts raised here.

Business Standard, December 28, 2006.

14 Seven *Minus* Seven *Equals* Seven?

One of the challenges for a regular columnist is to make each title interesting or, at least, a little mysterious, in the hope that the reader will be tempted to read on. Well, this one falls in the latter category. But too much mystery could be irritating, like those ultra-subtle French films where you have to desperately look for the solution of a whodunit in the closing long-shot. (I usually remain perplexed and have to ask someone.) So, let's cut to the chase. This piece is about seven reasons which explain India's extraordinary (and largely unexpected) 8.5 per cent economic growth in the last four years and seven reasons why this may not be sustained, suggesting that medium-term (next five years) growth is more likely to average around 7 per cent.

Success, they say, has a hundred fathers. My choice of the seven factors that explain India's exceptional recent growth are as follows: the cumulative, virtuous cycles embedded in 25 years of good (6 per cent) growth; the globalisation-reaping benefits of a much more open economy; an expanding "middle class" fuelling domestic consumption; the "demographic dividends" of a young population; the rise of strong companies in a modernised capital market; lower interest rates and an improving fisc; and strong global economic growth. A few words on each of these.

India is one of a handful of developing countries which has successfully averaged over 3 per cent per year per capita growth in the quarter century since 1980. Prolonged, steady growth triggers several virtuous cycles, including, especially, incentives for higher savings and investment.

Second, all that hard policy work in the 1990s of reducing customs tariffs, phasing out import licenses, moving to a market-responsive exchange rate and opening up to foreign capital has paid off handsomely in rewards from closer engagement with the world economy. Between 1990/91 and 2005/06 the ratio of foreign trade (goods) to GDP more than doubled from below 15 per cent to over 32 per cent, while the share of current receipts (goods exports plus invisible earnings) tripled from 8 per cent of GDP to 24 per cent. Basically, exports of goods and services (including software) have boomed, creating new jobs and raising productivity.

Third, the premature (in the early 1990s) hype about a growing middle class has, with growth, become much more of a reality, underpinning sustained and strong expansion of domestic demand. According to NCAER survey estimates, the number of people in households with annual incomes of Rs.2 to 10 lakhs has soared from around 15 million in 1990/91 to about 100 million in 2005/06. Hence, the explosive growth in sales of cars, two-wheelers, TVs, and of course, cell phones.

Fourth, the much-touted "demographic dividends" of India's young population may be oversold for its labour supply bulge (in a context of slow job growth), but the rising share of working age population has brought clear dividends in the form of growing household savings, which have helped finance higher national investment.

Fifth, the legal, institutional and technological reforms of India's capital markets in the 1990s have greatly assisted the rise of strong Indian companies, especially (but by no means exclusively) in sunrise industries of infotech, telecom, media, airlines, and pharma. An increasingly confident and competitive corporate sector has enhanced productivity and rapid investment growth.

Sixth, the fall in real interest rates in the early years of the decade and the more recent declines in Central and state deficits have also helped to induce and nurture the investment boom since 2003.

Finally, to the surprise of many forecasters, the world economy has powered ahead at almost 5 per cent over the last four years, propelled by strong growth in the US and China, and some recovery in Japan and Europe. India's now much more open economy has benefited from this global expansion.

Looking ahead, the seven key factors which are likely to constrain future growth are: renewed fiscal stress from populist policies, the perennial infrastructure bottlenecks, labour market rigidities, weak agricultural performance, slow economic reforms, weaknesses in human development programmes, and a possible slackening in global growth.

With general elections just two years away and the Sixth Pay Commission in train, the momentum of populist expenditure programmes is likely to gather steam, implying risks of renewed pressure on public deficits and savings, and consequent negative fall-out on investment and growth.

Second, the deficiencies in electric power, roads, water and urban infrastructure remain massive. Unless they are swiftly corrected, the Planning Commission's aspirations for nine per cent growth in the next five years look distinctly optimistic.

Third, without significant reforms of existing labour laws, India's cheap labour advantages will remain hugely unfulfilled. Moreover, with the bulk of the demographic bulge occurring in the weakly governed, poor and slow-growing states of central and eastern India, the challenge of ensuring broad-based, job-full growth is enormous.

Fourth, despite recent data revisions, the post-1996 record of agriculture remains disappointingly weak. Given the current state of systems of irrigation and water management, research, extension and credit, it is very hard to put faith in the four per cent agriculture growth projections of official planners. Indeed, secularly weak agricultural performance is a key factor sharpening the growth-inflation trade-off in the current environment.

Fifth, the slow-down in economic reforms over the past three years is an unwelcome reality. If reforms yield growth dividends with a lag, then the recent "reforms pause" could exact its toll from future growth.

Sixth, and in a longer time-frame, the woeful inadequacies in our public systems of education and healthcare (at all levels) are well-known. Their costs in terms of skill-development for an increasingly knowledge-driven and competitive world economy are uncertain but indubitably high in the long-run.

Lastly, the "Goldilocks" global expansion of the last few years cannot be taken for granted for ever. Those lurking bears could get nasty some time, with negative consequences for India's growth trajectory.

There you have it: the seven pluses and the seven minuses, so to speak. There is a good chance that the widely prevalent bullish expectations of 9-10 per cent growth in the medium-term are overly influenced by the recent past (2003 onwards), a period of strong cyclical upswing in both the global economy and Indian industry and services. Medium-term expectations for 7 per cent growth may seem unduly cautious today, but wiser with the benefit of hindsight. Any way, I prefer to be pleasantly surprised on the upside!

Business Standard, February 22, 2007.

15 The Rise of Indian Manufacturing?

Over the past year or two there has been mounting confidence about the new found strength of India's manufacturing sector and its long-term potential. The recently approved 11th Five Year Plan expects manufacturing to grow at 10-11 per cent a year during the period 2007-2012. Last week a business television channel posed the upbeat question "Does the next decade belong to manufacturing?" Earlier this month, Rakesh Mohan of RBI, in an otherwise very friendly review of my latest book, wrote (*Economic and Political Weekly*, December 8, 2007), "the resurgence of the manufacturing sector seems to have escaped Acharya's attention". Cut to the quick (though I am never sure which part of the anatomy is referred by this phrase), I decided to revisit the basic data on the sector. Here's what I found.

First, it's quite clear that from a global perspective India's manufacturing sector is quite modest in size. Thus in 2005, value added (or net output) of India's manufacturing amounted to only $115 billion as compared to $750 billion in China and over $1500 billion in the US. These comparisons are at official exchange rates (not at purchasing power parity rates) but that's entirely appropriate for a sector where the output is internationally tradable. As regards India-China comparisons, it's not just value added; manufactured exports are also seven times greater from China than India.

More interesting is the trajectory of India's manufacturing output over the last 15 years, covering three plan periods since the early 1990s reforms. Figure 15.1 and the accompanying table illustrate some salient points. First, the growth of manufacturing since 1991 has followed quite a roller-coaster profile. There was an initial post-reforms upswing in the mid-1990s, followed by a steep tumble in 1997/98, stagnation for the next four years and then a steady recovery and acceleration since 2002/03. In 5-year averages, manufacturing grew by a robust 9.5 per cent in the Eighth Plan (1992-1997), a lacklustre 3.3 per cent during the Ninth Plan (1997-2002), and a resurgent 8.7 per cent in the recently completed Tenth Plan (2002-2007).

Figure 15.1

Growth of Manufacturing Sector in India

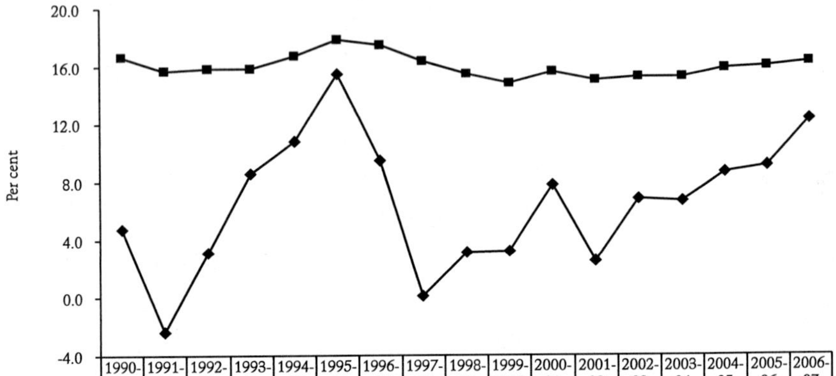

	1990-91	1991-92	1992-93	1993-94	1994-95	1995-96	1996-97	1997-98	1998-99	1999-2000	2000-01	2001-02	2002-03	2003-04	2004-05	2005-06	2006-07
◆ Growth	4.8	-2.4	3.1	8.6	10.8	15.5	9.5	0.1	3.1	3.2	7.7	2.5	6.8	6.6	8.7	9.1	12.3
■ Share in GDP	16.7	15.7	15.9	15.8	16.7	17.9	17.5	16.4	15.5	14.8	15.6	15.0	15.3	15.2	15.9	16.0	16.3

Source: CSO (*http://mospi.nic.in/mospi_cso_rept_pubn.htm*)

Second, the share of manufacturing in GDP has remained disappointingly flat, attaining a local peak of nearly 18 per cent in 1995/96 and a low of 15 per cent in 2001/02. At 16.3 per cent of GDP the share of manufacturing in 2006/07 was still below the 16.7 per cent level of 1990/91. In contrast, the share of services (even excluding construction) in GDP has risen steadily during this period from 44 per cent to 55 per cent. This stagnation in the share of manufacturing is very different from the experience of successful East Asian economies. A comparison with China is very unfavourable to India: in 2005, China's manufacturing share in GDP of 34 per cent was more than double of India's.

What about future prospects? Optimists believe that while the mid-1990s industrial boom was a temporary spurt propelled by the early 1990s freeing of industrial and trade controls, the more recent, post-2002 resurgence is much more firmly grounded in an internationally competitive and confident manufacturing sector, which has internalised capabilities for sustained, strong corporate performance and buoyant investment. They point out that in the past three years manufacturing averaged growth of just over 10 per cent a year. Against that background the Eleventh Plan's expectation of 10-11 per cent growth for the next five years should be an easy target. Indeed, they expect faster growth and a steadily rising share of manufacturing in GDP.

Well, maybe. But let me raise a few doubts for the optimists. First, the period 2001-2007 witnessed an unexpectedly strong performance of the global economy, led by a powerful, import-intensive boom in the US. With each passing month there is a growing consensus that the "sub-prime"-triggered credit crunch in industrial economies will slow the US and global growth significantly in the next couple of years. If that were to happen, Indian industry is unlikely to remain unscathed, notwithstanding the popular, but untested, theories of "decoupling". Second, an important stimulus to the recent, strong manufacturing growth has come from a surge in corporate investment activity. Can this be sustained for long? Has India outgrown the vagaries of business cycles? The graph is none too reassuring. Third, the momentum of manufacturing growth could be significantly dented by our exchange rate policy, which has been mismanaged since March this year (see my piece in *Business Standard* of November 8, 2007). Labour-intensive exports and import-substitutes are already hurting. More pain may well be in store if the appreciation of the rupee is not curbed.

Fourth, we have been enjoying a benign period of declining fiscal deficits in the last five years. That particular joyride is threatened by a number of factors, including: the mounting off-budget subsidies for oil, food, and fertilisers, the ticking time-bomb of the Sixth Pay Commission, rising expenditure on various populist programmes and a possible slowdown in the rapid growth of corporate income taxes. If fiscal deficits widen again, upward pressure on interest rates and (downward on) investment is inevitable. Finally, progress in releasing our infrastructure constraints remain painfully slow, especially in power, water, roads, and urban services. How long before this takes its toll of manufacturing sector dynamism?

What can government policy do to improve the medium and long-term prospects for the manufacturing sector? Quite a lot, though none of it is particularly novel. First, in the short run, macroeconomic policy should be calibrated to curb the appreciation of the rupee. Second, every effort should be made to hang on to the hard won gains of fiscal consolidation, including through necessary hikes in domestic prices of petroleum products. Third, the usual agenda of infrastructure reforms would pay high dividends for manufacturing productivity and competitiveness. Fourth, reform of our labour laws would encourage scaling up production levels in manufacturing units in labour-intensive industries such as textiles, garments, and leather products, thereby increasing output, exports and employment in these sectors. Finally, for the longer run, there is a whole raft of measures that need to be adopted in education, training, and health to enhance the productivity of our labour force and generate the kind of skill mixes sought by an expanding industrial sector. It's all been said before, with dubious impact on actual policy!

Business Standard, December 27, 2007.

16 The Halcyon Years, 2003-2008

Gloom and doom is the prevailing mood as the world of global finance comes tumbling down and levies substantial collateral damage on global economic prosperity. Instead of one more sombre article on this now familiar theme, let me swim against the tide for a while and celebrate India's economic prosperity of the past five years, 2003/04 to 2007/08. In doing so, I also hope to meet the criticism of some friends that my columns tend to dwell too much on the dark side of things (Darth Vader rest in peace). Actually, this complaint comes mostly from my Punjabi friends who are usually brimming with incorrigible optimism and gusto (even when the sky is about to fall down) and cannot sympathise too easily with my Bengali pessimism. After the Singur-Nano fiasco, they may better understand why we Bongs tend to attach low probabilities to good outcomes.

Most people know about India's stellar economic growth in the past five years, at a scorching average annual rate of 8.8 per cent (If they don't, the finance ministry and planning commission will be happy to send them the data in multi-media). That's a full third faster than the next best five year period in the country's recorded history, namely in the immediate post-reform quinquennium of 1992-1997, when the average growth clocked 6.6 per cent (see Table 16.1).

Table 16.1

Macro Overview Comparison

	(1) *1992/93-1996/97*	*(2)* *1997/98-2001/02*	*(3)* *2003/04-2007/08*
Economic Growth (% per year)	6.6	5.5	8.8
Inflation (GDP deflator, % per year)	9.1	5.0	4.5
Current Account Deficit (% of GDP)	1.1	0.6	0.4
Combined Fiscal Deficit (% of GDP)	7.1	9.0	6.7
Gross Domestic Investment (% of GDP)	24.2	24.3	33.6

What may be less well appreciated is India's exceptionally strong performance on all the other major parameters of macroeconomic performance as well in the last five years. The average rate of inflation, measured by the conceptually best available indicator, the GDP deflator, was only 4.5 per cent in 2003-2008, half the rate recorded in 1992-1997 and even lower than the inflation rate in the intervening slow growth period of 1997-2002. The most preferred single indicator of the health of a country's external balance is the current account deficit. In 2003-2008 this averaged only 0.4 per cent of GDP, lower than in any other five-year period in the last 30 years.

Fiscal balance (or lack of it) is usually the commonest indicator of domestic balance in an economy, next to inflation. Since 1980, India has been a high deficit country, confounding *pundits* from international institutions and rating agencies by her capacity, nevertheless, to turn in strong growth and modest inflation. In 1997-2002 (post Fifth Pay Commission) the combined deficit of the Centre and states had risen to an unsustainably high 9 per cent of GDP. By 2003-2008, corrective action by the Centre and states brought the fiscal deficit down substantially to 6.7 per cent of GDP, even lower than the level achieved in 1992-1997. Perhaps even more remarkable is India's investment performance in recent years. Gross domestic investment jumped to a record 34 per cent of GDP in 2003-2008, from a much lower plateau of 24 per cent in both 1992-1997 and 1997-2002. This massive investment boom was both a cause and consequence of the nation's extraordinary growth in recent years.

What explains India's outstanding macroeconomic performance in these halcyon years? Better scholars than I will research and debate this question for many years to come and one day there may be a consensus. For now, let me present my top five candidates for "the most important causes" of this exceptional economic performance. First, the cumulative reforms between 1991 and 2004 were absolutely crucial in releasing the country's latent dynamism and reaping the benefits of foreign trade and capital flows. Not many reforms occurred in 2004-2008, for which we will pay the price in future. Indeed, reform thrusts were rolled back in some areas, such as privatisation, oil pricing, tax policy, and interest rate controls. However, in one very important dimension, the present government did achieve a lot, in bringing about major reductions in the fiscal and revenue deficits of Central and state governments. These reductions constitute my second of the "prime causes" for the economic boom, for they engendered a massive improvement in public savings, a large increase in loanable funds for productive investment and significantly lower real interest rates.

The third major factor was the remarkable (and unexpected) global economic expansion of 2002-2007, which vindicated the benefits of globalisation (of trade, technology and capital flows) by pumping up growth in many countries, including India. Fourth, for a change, India caught the bus on the global services boom, racking up rapid growth not just in software exports but in a wide range of services, including telecom, media, finance, and retail. Last, but by no means least, India's excellent macroeconomic performance was nurtured by the exceptionally deft exchange rate management and monetary policy conducted by the Reserve Bank in unusually challenging circumstances. In particular, the challenge of surging foreign capital inflows was adroitly managed without undue damage to a competitive exchange rate policy, so crucial for sustaining the boom in exports of goods and services.

"Halcyon" is an adjective usually deployed for times gone by. Its use in this piece is no exception. By March 2008 the global commodity price shock had sent India's inflation soaring skywards. With prices of oil, fertilisers, and foodgrains held down by government, sharply rising international prices meant massive and rising subsidies, which sent the hard-won achievements of fiscal consolidation for a six and took the foreign trade deficit to 10 per cent of GDP. Attempts to disguise the yawning fiscal deficit through devices such as oil and fertiliser bonds proved ill-conceived and useless. As India struggled with high inflation and rising fiscal and external imbalances, the festering sub-prime-based international credit crisis exploded in September, capital inflows reversed sharply, liquidity became scarce and the spectre of a major international recession clouded India's growth prospects (these developments are analysed in my series of articles in *Business Standard* of June 26, August 14, and September 25).

So, the nasty global shocks of the last eight months have brought a swift end to my brief flirtation with Punjabi optimism. The ambient mood is more suited to my natural disposition. Growth is slowing to 7.5 per cent (if we are lucky) this year and perhaps below 7 per cent in 2009/10. Inflation, measured by the WPI, is in double digits for several months now. The current account deficit in the balance of payments is likely to be 3 to 4 per cent of GDP. The combined true fiscal deficit may be 9 to 10 per cent of GDP. And the investment rate is bound to drop. But, even as the economic indicators turn inexorably negative, let us not forget those halcyon years. Who knows when (or if) they will return.

Business Standard, October 9, 2008.

IV

Financial Sector

17 The Mystery Report

One fine October morning, nearly 36 years ago, two young Indians landed up at the personnel department (now would be called HR) of the World Bank in Washington to sign on for the Bank's Young Professional Programme. One was Percy Mistry, the erstwhile chairman of the High Powered Expert Committee (HPEC) on developing Mumbai as an international financial centre (IFC). The other was me. Percy and I have been friends since then, although our very different trajectories in life and geography have constrained the closeness of our friendship. I sincerely hope that the ensuing critical appraisal of the HPEC report will not strain our amity. However, knowing Percy's largeness of heart and mind, I am fairly sanguine on this score.

Percy is a no-nonsense sort of fellow. So I was not altogether surprised to learn that he had resigned the chairmanship of HPEC a few days before the report was submitted to the finance minister in early February. It certainly created a piquant, if not mysterious, situation. According to the grapevine and the press, the final draft of the report had contained scathing references to the performance and problems of public sector banks (PSBs), which provoked the PSB bank chiefs on HPEC (who had been largely absent in earlier meetings of the committee) to demand alterations of the draft. Percy refused and quit. The report was diluted and submitted to the government. More on this later.

The HPEC report is a curious mixture of interesting analysis, some blatant financial sector boosterism, a few significant diagnostic weaknesses and a long and motley list of policy recommendations, including some sensible and some bizarre ones. Taking the positives first, the report provides very useful discussions and definitions of IFCs and IFS (international financial services). It goes on to list key requirements for successful development of an IFC and notes that Mumbai possesses several of the necessary attributes, such as a fast growing hinterland generating expanding demand for IFS, good human capital, good location, democracy and rule of law, and quite well-developed securities markets. On the flip side, the report identifies key gaps, which need to be filled if Mumbai is to successfully aspire to develop into a thriving IFC.

These include: weak financial governance, missing markets (such as for bonds and derivatives) and institutions (such as large international and domestic institutional investors), and the poor urban infrastructure of Mumbai. The report goes on to analyse these shortcomings in some detail and then presents a long and daunting list of policy prescriptions.

HPEC fails to make a clear and compelling case for the benefits flowing from nurturing Mumbai into an IFC. It asserts: " In sustaining its trajectory as an emerging, globally significant, continental economy,...India has no choice but to (a) become a producer and exporter of IFS; and (b) capture an increasing share of the rapidly growing global IFS market. To achieve these two goals, its financial centre in Mumbai *must* become a successful IFC." This is simply an assertion, not the conclusion of a reasoned argument. It's also wrong. Just look at the striking development successes of East Asia and Southern Europe post-1960. Barring the city states of Singapore and Hong Kong, having (or developing) an IFC was not a "must" for the tremendously successful economic development trajectories of Korea, Malaysia, Taiwan, Thailand, China, Spain, Portugal, and Greece.

The mere fact that India might purchase around $50 billion of IFS by 2015 (HPEC projections) constitutes no case for their local production. By then, India will quite likely be importing $800-1,000 billion of goods and services. That's an outcome of healthy international specialisation and commerce, not a case for producing everything in India. There is no shame in importing sizeable amounts of IFS, if India does not have a comparative advantage to produce or export them.

Perhaps the most obvious diagnostic soft-pedalling (dilution of the draft?) concerns the regulatory weakness stemming from the dominance of government-owned financial institutions. HPEC correctly observes, "The quality and credibility of IFS provided from India is inextricably linked to the soundness and global acceptability of the regulatory/legal system that governs finance in India." Yet, to take the most obvious example, banks constitute the biggest part of India's financial system and three-quarters of banking assets are in PSBs. How can the RBI seriously improve its regulation of PSBs when the owner (the government) outranks the regulator? And, one might add, frequently issues diktats to both RBI and PSBs, not to mention packing PSB boards with political hacks. The mystery report does contain gentle references to the need for "diminished public presence" and "reduced equity stake" of government. But there is no clarion call for tackling the 800lb gorilla in India's financial living room, which squats athwart the path of regulatory reform. Basically, without privatisation of PSBs and government insurance companies, the chances of developing an IFC in Mumbai are dim.

HPEC favours radical reforms in India's financial regulatory architecture, including "unifying all organized financial trading under SEBI regulation... including currencies...". As a relatively young regulator, SEBI has done rather well in evolving stock market regulation. But extending its domain to currencies, commodity derivatives and so forth seems premature at best, and unwise, at worst. Given RBI's much longer regulatory history and (unlike SEBI) trained cadres, a more pluralistic approach to regulatory architecture seems safer for the foreseeable future. Indeed, HPEC displays surprising insensitivity to the historical and contextual contours of financial regulation in India.

Another key diagnostic weakness of HPEC lies in blithely recommending rapid transition to full capital account convertibility (CAC), without adequately considering the implied loss of autonomy for India's exchange rate and monetary policies. HPEC shows little understanding of the nuances and benefits of an "intermediate" exchange rate regime of the kind that has served India well for over 15 years (see my article, *Business Standard*, April 26). Perhaps this is because the HPEC's composition was long on finance chiefs and short on policy economists.

The mystery report lists 48 (!) "Recommended Actions" (mostly in the next two years) for paving the way for Mumbai's rise as an IFC. It's a wide-ranging and challenging list. Given space constraints, I have listed a few of these in Table 17.1 and added my telegraphic comment on each. I have omitted most of a long list of prescriptions to improve Mumbai as an urban centre (a worthy goal in itself). With Maharashtra's power system in shambles and brown-outs looming over Mumbai, the IFC vision seems distant. Indeed, after pondering HPEC's policy prescriptions I am inclined to conclude that the chances of Mumbai emerging as an IFC within a decade or so are somewhat less than my becoming a concert pianist (and I haven't started my lessons yet!).

Table 17.1

Selected HPEC Recommendations

Recommendation Actions	Comment
• Achieving and maintaining growth rate of 9% to 10%	An action? An objective surely.
• Reduce gross consolidated fiscal deficit to 4-5% of GDP by 2010	Welcome, but achievable?
• Restructure budgets of states and municipal corporations by 2010	Welcome, but achievable?
• Full capital account convertibility by end 2008	Much too fast for sound macro policy
• GoI to reduce equity stake in all financial firms to 26% by 2010	Welcome, but highly unlikely
• Create International Financial Services Appellate Tribunal by 2010	"Sovereignty" concerns could block
• Permit free entry of well-known global legal firms by 2009	Domestic lobby could block
• Permit free entry of well-known global accounting firms by 2009	Domestic lobby could block
• Shift financial regulation from "rules-based" to "principles-based" by 2010	Welcome, in principle
• Transfer all regulation/supervision of organised financial trading to SEBI by 2008	Premature; perhaps unwise
• Foreign bank branches freely licensed after mid-2008	Needs gradual phasing
• GoM and BMC to appoint Mumbai City Manager by 2008	Highly unlikely
• Full control of city governance machinery by City Manager by 2009	

Business Standard, May 24, 2007.

18 The New Orthodoxy Crumbles

Over the past two decades a new orthodoxy has evolved regarding the governance and conduct of financial regulation/supervision and monetary policy. While the subject is complex and has plenty of nuances, it would be fair to say that the new orthodoxy is based on three key pillars: first, a nation's central bank should be accorded statutory independence from government; second, the central bank should be charged with the single (or primary) target of keeping inflation low; and third, all financial trading and intermediaries should be brought under a separate single regulator. This orthodoxy gained a lot of ground over the last 20 years in the industrial economies of Australia, the UK, the US, Europe, and Japan. In these economies (which had adopted the new orthodoxy to somewhat different degrees) the new system seemed to work pretty well and developing countries, such as India, were increasingly urged to move the new model, not least by some enthusiastic domestic commentators.

The notorious and still unfolding "sub-prime" mortgage crisis and its credit crunch aftermath last month in the US and other major OECD economies have blown a few holes in the new orthodoxy. It's useful to review the salient points and try to distill some lessons for India's monetary/financial policy in today's turbulent financial world.

The UK provides perhaps the best example of a wholesale shift to the new orthodoxy as well as some of the key weaknesses recent events have exposed. Within a few weeks of coming to power in 1997 the new Labour government's chancellor of the exchequer, Gordon Brown, implemented the three key pillars of the new orthodoxy in the UK. The Bank of England (BoE) was made independent. It was fully mandated to pursue the primary objective of inflation control, with explicit inflation targeting. The Bank's supervisory/regulatory functions were taken away and given to the newly established Financial Services Authority (FSA). For a decade the new system worked fine. Then, this September, as the ramifications of the US sub-prime crisis unfolded, it all came apart when the brave new ship of the new orthodoxy ran aground on the Northern Rock, the UK's fifth biggest mortgage bank.

The events are well known and need no recounting. But the crisis did raise serious questions about the new orthodoxy. Can you really have an independent central bank when "the mother of central banks", the BoE, was seen to reverse its public stance within a matter of days, apparently under severe pressure from the government? In mid-September, the governor, Mervyn King, was extolling tough central banking scriptures about not bailing out imprudent financiers. Within a few short days he was doing just that, while the UK Treasury was guaranteeing bank deposits (and to hell with the doctrine of discouraging "moral hazard"). Like it or not, financial stability and maintaining economic activity had become the primary concerns of the BoE, with inflation targeting put on the back burner. Nor did the FSA escape unscathed. Its supervision of Northern Rock had clearly been far from perfect. Questions were also raised about the separation of the supervision function (with FSA) from the task of providing emergency accommodation (with BoE).

Across the Atlantic, the Federal Reserve's actions also demonstrated pretty obviously that low inflation was only one of its major objectives. The reduction of the Fed's discount rate, the loosening of collateral provisions and the half per cent cut in the Fed Funds rate in September, all clearly showed that Governor Bernanke and his colleagues accorded great importance to the other worthy objectives of preserving financial stability and maintaining the rate of US economic activity. Indeed, these three objectives of low inflation, financial stability and maintaining economic activity close to potential are really no different from the RBI's stated objectives. And it should not be surprising that, in fact, if not in rhetoric, serious central banks give major weight to all three. It's only the acolytes of the new orthodoxy who get carried away by the slogan of "inflation control as the sole objective".

If vindication of multiple objectives for sound central banking is one lesson of the recent crisis, what are some others? What about the doctrine of independence for central banks? Well, the September crisis in the UK suggests that whatever the legislation or the professed doctrines, in a crunch, the Leviathan (the government) tends to prevail. That does not mean good central banking should abandon the principle of autonomy and independence. It just means that in the real world such independence can never be absolute, and especially not in crunch situations. In India, with a relatively undeveloped culture and conventions for conferring true autonomy (from government) to public institutions, there may be still a case for legal amendments to enhance the RBI's independence. But such efforts should not feed the illusion of absolute independence.

How about the much hyped "single regulator" model? Have recent events discredited it? My sense is that the jury is still out on this one. In any particular country, what may matter more is not the form of the model prevailing (single *vs.* multiple regulators) but how well or badly it is worked and coordinated with the central bank and government by the incumbents and how much real acceptance the structure commands in the financial community and, more broadly, the larger society and polity. These are as much (or more) a product of institutional history and political/administrative culture as the organograms of particular models. In India, I think it would be premature, at present, to expect much success with the FSA type single regulator model. Besides, with our weak and unwieldy coalition governments, who has the stomach for the required legislative overhaul?

Finally, the sub-prime crisis and its credit-freezing aftermath have shown that even very mature and established central banks, financial supervision authorities and the respective governments of rich, industrialised nations resort to somewhat eclectic and *ad hoc* solutions and responses when confronted with unforeseen and serious, systemic financial problems. Against this background it should be easier to sympathise with the Indian authorities' recent and somewhat untidy efforts to grapple with the unprecedented surge in foreign capital inflows and their destabilising consequences. The shrill and simplistic critiques of over-zealous "market fundamentalists" are not very helpful. Nor, of course, is blind defence of any and all public regulatory interventions.

Business Standard, October 25, 2007.

19 The Rajan Report on Finance

The draft report of the committee on financial sector reform, chaired by Raghuram Rajan (professor of finance, Chicago Business School), has been placed on a website and comments have been invited. I am accepting this invitation with some trepidation. Last year, when Percy Mistry persuaded me to do a column on his "Mumbai as an International Finance Centre" report, he got a bit huffy when I mixed my praise with a few criticisms. Raghu, I expect, is made of sterner stuff. That emboldens me to use the limited space of this column to focus on some of the key weaknesses of the draft Raghuram Rajan Report (henceforth RRR), while recognising that there is much that is sensible and interesting in the document.

To begin with, there is a structural flaw in the committee's composition. And I am not referring to the heavy dominance of finance wizards over representatives of the real economy (none) and macroeconomists (one). Far more important is the total absence of senior people from either the RBI or the Finance Ministry. Indian experience suggests that there is serious follow through on financial sector reports only when both MoF and RBI "own" the document. If composition is any guide, that may not happen here. But that's water under the bridge. Let's turn to substance.

RRR's treatment of the "macroeconomic framework" is curiously academic and aloof from the realities of the Indian macroeconomic setting and experience. There seems to be little understanding of the potential and possibilities of macroeconomic policy in a developing country with an "intermediate" exchange rate regime of managed flexibility and partial capital controls. This might have been excusable if India's macroeconomic outcomes in terms of growth and inflation had been bad in recent years. In fact, of course, India has done remarkably well in comparison to all developing countries. So, monetary and exchange rate management couldn't have been as bad as RRR's calls for system change suggest (contra the old adage "if it ain't broke, don't fix it").

To take just one example, RRR believes that capital inflows lead to inevitable appreciation of the real exchange rate, leaving the country with "the Hobson's choice of taking it as inflation or nominal exchange rate appreciation." This view is, at best, misleading and, at worst, plain wrong. The third and better option, pursued by government and RBI (except in spring 2007), has been to add to forex reserves and partially sterilise the increment (note that in recent years RBI has added well over $200 billion of reserves while the cumulative MSS bonds outstanding is a little over $40 billion equivalent). This avoids unwanted nominal and real appreciation of the exchange rate as well as inflationary pressure. Of course, sterilisation imposes fiscal costs but most studies indicate they are a small fraction of the real GDP costs exacted by an over-appreciated exchange rate.

RRR's narrow view of macroeconomics leads it to a surprisingly adventurist recommendation: that "RBI should have a single objective...of low inflation...". It's one thing for youthful columnists to peddle a recent academic fashion. It's quite another for a serious, high level committee to make this their first recommendation. Just consider what this means: that the RBI should drop the other objectives which currently also inform its policies, namely, the level and growth of the country's economic activity, the nation's financial stability and the level and volatility of the exchange rate, which is generally regarded as the single most important price in a developing country. RRR is not particularly educative on who should take on these responsibilities and how, especially given the well-known constraints on counter-cyclical fiscal policy in India. This is not to deny that the model of an inflation-targeting central bank may have worked in some (mostly developed) countries at some times. It's simply to recognise its obvious inappropriateness for current (and medium-term) Indian conditions. Note also that the world's largest economy with, arguably, the most developed financial system, the US, mandates its central bank to pursue multiple objectives. Nor was the Bank of England solely focused on targeting inflation when it announced various policies to cope with the Northern Rock fiasco last autumn.

Turning to RRR's discussion of the regulatory structure, I am pleased that it has resisted the siren song of the "single regulator" model. Unfortunately, it has submitted a couple of weird proposals. The first is for a statutory Financial Sector Oversight Agency (FSOA), composed of "chiefs of regulatory bodies" and armed with a "permanent secretariat" to "monitor...large, systemically important financial conglomerates,...defuse inter-regulatory conflicts", etc. RRR hugely underestimates the dangers of spawning a new regulatory institution in a country which loves such multiplication and where bureaucratic turf battles usually take precedence over problem-solving. If the issue is inter-regulatory coordination, it's not obvious that an FSOA will provide anything more than another venue for discord. A better solution, generally favoured the world over, is to accord primary authority to the central bank and sort out coordination and overlap issues through semi-formal institutions such as the High Level Committee on the Capital Market (chaired by the RBI Governor), with occasional recourse to the finance minister to resolve particularly knotty issues.

I have similar qualms about the proposed Financial Development Council (FDC), to be chaired by the finance minister, to handle "macro risk assessment and developmental issues". Once again, the danger is of bureaucratisation and excessive governmental control over relatively autonomous financial sector regulatory institutions. Better to stick with the present system where ministerial direction and guidance is conveyed through less structured channels. Incidentally, it would be good to know which other countries boast similar institutions (as the proposed FSOA and FDC) and how they have worked in practice. Or is India to be RRR's guinea pig?

Similarly, the proposal for more formal parliamentary oversight of time-bound, structured mandates to regulators may lead to far more pervasive and intrusive political intervention in the discharge of professional regulatory responsibilities than RRR may have foreseen. My suggestion would be to tread very cautiously in this domain.

In pursuit of the worthy goal of greater financial inclusion, RRR recommends resurrection of small, local area private banks. The dangers of capture by local private-political vested interests are noted by RRR, but it nevertheless considers the initiative worthwhile. I wonder if RRR may have underestimated the enormous regulatory challenges involved, especially in a multi(in dozens!)-party federation with declining governance standards. Just recall the checkered history of urban cooperative banks.

These are some of my concerns with the rich and provocative agenda for change proposed by RRR. Long years have taught me not to expect significant report revisions as a result of comments. Never mind. I have done my *dharma*.

Business Standard, April 10, 2008.

V

Fiscal Policy

20 Reality Rules

What do you do if you are the reform-oriented Finance Minister in an unwieldy coalition government which rules with Left "support" (with friends like these, who needs enemies!) and honour bound to follow a fiscal consolidation path mandated by the FRBM Act that your government notified less than three years ago? You can't announce big ticket reforms like amendment of restrictive labour laws or privatisation of government banks, oil and coal companies. After all, even the modest reforms of pensions and FDI limits in insurance and retail that you announced in earlier years remain stalled by your political "supporters". You don't want to stray from the architecture of tax policy that your own Prime Minister ushered in 15 years ago and which successive FMs (including yourself) of different governments have bought into and built upon. You can't even launch too many wild expenditure schemes (anyway you wouldn't want to) thanks to the constraints of the fiscal responsibility law.

So what do you do? The short and truthful answer is ...not much, which is exactly what Mr. Chidambaram has done in this budget. The somewhat longer answer is as follows. First, you describe, in numbing detail, your budget allocations for education and health and other social sectors (on ongoing schemes), while eliding over the fact that the cutting edge of these programmes are the responsibility of state governments. You spend the next 20 minutes of your budget speech talking about agriculture and rural development, referring to various ongoing programmes but being careful not to announce any really big (and possibly misguided) new scheme. Then you announce the expansion of that dubious National Rural Employment Guarantee Scheme to 130 new districts, thus making a virtue of the internal battle you recently lost to contain the expansion of this misconceived and expensive gravy train to fewer districts. (You don't say anything about how well or badly this massive scheme has fared in the first 200 districts where it was launched a year back; but then, who cares about outcomes?) By now you have established you are PC...in more ways than one.

So now you can turn to tax reform, the stuff that industry, the pink papers and economists lap up. The problem here is that most of the serious tax reform has already been done in the last 20 years by your predecessors: V.P. Singh, Manmohan Singh, Yashwant Sinha and yourself (1996-97 edition). Just compare the tax structure of Sinha's 2001 budget and yours of now: same Cenvat general rate of 16 per cent; same corporate rate of 30 per cent, same personal income tax structure of 10-20-30 (with minor add-ons of surcharge and cess). The big changes are the reduction of the peak customs duty rate from 35 to 10 per cent (your four budgets have managed a reduction from 20 to 10) and the large expansion in services taxes and increases in the rate. Indeed, this remarkable continuity and stability in the basic architecture of India's tax policy is a tribute to the above pantheon of FMs and their advisers.

Actually, there *are* two big areas for tax reform that beckon. One is the full integration of excise (commodity) taxes with the services tax. But that would involve raising the rate of tax on services from the present 12 per cent towards a general Cenvat rate, possibly dropped to 15 or 14 per cent. In a politically charged, inflationary environment you decide to duck that one. The other, of course, is the roadmap for a national level goods and services tax that had been recommended by the Kelkar committee in 2004 and which you announced last year. But you find that your officials haven't made much progress in cartography. So you simply reannounce the desirability of the roadmap!

Finally you (being you) can't resist a few offbeat and "clever" little tax initiatives. Like the dual rate tax on cement. Like the extension of fringe benefit tax (FBT) to ESOPs. Like the application of services tax to commercial property rentals (that should kiss goodbye to Mumbai as a regional financial centre!). The problem with these ploys is that they may seem clever but are basically unsound and counter-productive to the goal of healthy economic development.

Overall, this budget won't make much difference to India's economic growth or inflation. Nor will it bring about any revolution in agriculture, infrastructure or social sector services. All that takes much longer and sustained effort at all levels of government, not just the annual central budget. And it calls for serious administrative reform and accountability, which are not mentioned in the budget speech.

So there you have it, my friends. In the 21st century you just have to get used to dull, real (not "dream") budgets. Irrespective of content, supporters will call them growth-oriented and anti-inflationary, while opponents will damn them as inflationary and anti-growth! The sober truth is that any decent budget won't make waves. If you want waves, go to Goa.

Outlook, March 12, 2007.

21 The Tenth of the Fifth

Yes, this month is the tenth anniversary of the United Front (UF) government's profligate decisions on the report of the Fifth Pay Commission (FPC). It's an event worth recalling (though not celebrating) for at least two reasons. First, these decisions had serious adverse consequences for India's economy and public finances lasting through most of the Ninth Plan period (1997-2002). Second, with the Sixth Pay Commission (SPC) launched last year and its report expected in late 2008 or early 2009, it is interesting to speculate about the possible outcome, which could impact significantly on India's future development trajectory.

Back in 2001, I wrote "the FPC effects constitute the single largest adverse shock to India's strained public finances in the last decade, with corresponding negative consequences for aggregate savings and investment in the economy." Six years later I stand by that assessment. The September 1997 decisions resulted in pay and pension increases of 40 per cent and higher to Central government employees, which were soon emulated by state governments. Importantly, the pay and pension increases decided by the government were much higher than those recommended by the FPC for the vast majority of employees. The sociology of the decision-making was simple. The FPC had recommended the large increases of 40 per cent plus for the executive grades of the government system (exemplified by the IAS/IFS/IPS, etc.) and much lower increases for the vast majority of lower rank employees (even by the most liberal definitions the "executive grades" account for less than 5 per cent of government employees). This is because the FPC judged government executives to be underpaid relative to comparators in the private sector but deemed this not to be the case for the vast majority of government employees (such as clerks, peons, service workers, teachers, etc).

Confronted by union pressure the UF government succumbed and accorded the large increases to virtually all government employees, with the unfortunate consequences that reverberated for several years. At the macro level, the combined fiscal deficit of Centre and states rose from 6.4 per cent of GDP in 1996/97 to 9.9 per cent in 2001/02, while the revenue deficit (a close approximation of government dissavings) doubled from 3.6 per cent of GDP in 1996/97 to 7 per cent in 2001/02 (Table 21.1). About half of this fiscal deterioration was directly attributable to the FPC decisions. As I have pointed out elsewhere (*Business Standard*, 30 November 2006), the marked worsening of the fiscal position was a notable cause behind the deceleration of economic growth in the period 1997-2002 , following the post-reforms boom of 1992-1997. Conversely, the growth surge of 2002-2007 has been helped significantly by the fiscal consolidation of recent years.

There were other major adverse effects of the FPC decisions. The perennially stressed finances of state governments became much worse. Rising pay and pension obligations pre-empted spending on material and investment inputs for education, health, roads and other basic infrastructure. Thus, the actual public service provision and development capacities of state governments suffered enormously during these years and it is doubtful whether they have recovered fully in the present decade. Second, the FPC-driven pay increases worsened the dualism in India's labour markets (Table 21.2). For example, it

Table 21.1

Combined Deficits of Central and State Governments

(As a Percentage of GDP)

Indicator	*1990/91*	*1996/97*	*2001/02*	*2006/07*
Gross Fiscal Deficit	9.4	6.4	9.9	6.4
Revenue Deficit	4.2	3.6	7.0	2.1
Gross Primary Deficit	5.0	1.3	3.7	0.8

Source: RBI, *Handbook of Statistics on Indian Economy*, September 2006 and Annual Report, 2006/07.

Table 21.2

Ratio of Average Wages in the Public over the Private Sector for Selected Categories of Employment

Occupation	*1993/94*	*1999/2000*
Administrative, Executive, and Managerial Workers	1.26	1.42
Teachers	1.75	2.02
Stenographers and Typists	1.69	2.14
General Clerks (receptionists, office attendants)	1.54	1.72
Service Workers	2.25	2.45
Sweepers, Cleaners, and Building Caretakers	1.79	1.93

Source: World Bank (2003), *India: Sustaining Reform, Reducing Poverty*, Oxford University Press, New Delhi.

widened the gap between the pay of government school teachers and those appointed by local communities and private institutions, thus stunting the incentives for non-government initiatives for provision of social services. Third, by transferring about 1.5 per cent of GDP to about 3 per cent of the country's labour force (government employees and all in the "formal sector") the FPC decisions probably worsened income inequality in India and were no help to the poor. Fourth, government pay increases led to similar increases in public sector units and probably strengthened the vested interests against the policies of disinvestment and privatisation.

Alright, the FPC decisions took a substantial toll of India's development momentum and fiscal health for several years. What of the future? What can we expect from the SPC and the decisions on their recommendations? As regards the latter, that is, the government's decisions on prospective SPC recommendations, the only thing it may be safe to conclude is that the government of the day (most likely another unwieldy coalition) is very likely to decide pay increases in excess of whatever recommendations the SPC makes. And what might those be? Obviously, we will only know when the SPC report becomes available. Till then we can only speculate. Let me voice my main concern.

It seems to me that the main new factor that has emerged in the past decade, and especially in the last six or seven years, is the dynamism of India's private corporate sector and the sharp increases in corporate executive remuneration. Never mind that the corporate world in India is highly diverse and there are a huge number of small struggling companies with ill-paid executives. The dominant impression, fanned by the press and TV, is one of super salaries in large, fast-growing companies. Against this background the SPC will be under heavy pressure to recommend large pay increases for executive grades of government employees, probably even more so than in 1996. If that happens, it's hard to see how India can avoid another large fiscal shock with the kind of unfortunate chain of economic consequences that resulted from the FPC. Even if the recommended pay increases for the 95 per cent plus of "non-executive" government employees are modest, the sociology of decision-making that occurred with the FPC recommendations is quite likely to prevail again. If government "executives" get X per cent increase, then that is likely to be the realistic increment for *all* employees. And then we shall see a rerun of the negative economic and public finance consequences that were triggered by the FPC decisions.

At least, that's my worry. I hope the esteemed members of the SPC will prove me wrong with their report.

Business Standard, September 27, 2007.

22 Year of the Carp

A fortnight has passed since the Union budget was presented. As usual, it has provoked reams of commentary from serried ranks of financial journalists, tax consultants, investment analysts, general columnists and, of course, my own tribe...economists. Reviewing the flood of material that has been published, I am struck by the apparent disconnect between the views of the general run of commentators (GC, for short), who have broadly welcomed the budget, *versus* the economists tribe, who have been mainly critical (see, for example, the views of six economists in the latest *India Today*). Why this disconnect between carping economists (CE) and the other professional commentators? The following platonic dialogue between a fictional representative of each group tries to shed some light.

GC: Hey, man, that was a really good budget, wasn't it? FM has made all the big vote banks happy: farmers, urban middle class, *aam admi*, and the poor. And he has done it without sacrificing fiscal prudence. He has even thrown in some reform stuff for you reform-*wallahs*. You have got to hand it him. He has pulled off the impossible: a sound budget with enormous political appeal. What more could you have asked from him? A Bharat Ratna for sure!

CE: Well...I concede it's a clever, political budget. But it's not that good when you look at it carefully. Let's take a look at the four major dimensions of the budget: reform announcements; overall fiscal stance; expenditure priorities, and tax measures. Take reforms first. There's no forward movement on the big ticket reform needs of the country such as power sector overhaul, privatisation of banking and energy companies, major subsidies, labour laws, agricultural policy, education, retail trade and so forth...

GC: Come on, *yaar*! Be reasonable. You know perfectly well that the Lefties and the Congress old guard have blocked all these reforms for the last four years. What do you expect FM to do about it? Besides, he has given you some tax reform and something about "bond, currency and derivative markets". Boy, you economists are really mean! Any way, let's move on to your "fiscal stance" yardstick. He has really hit a sixer there. Even bigger than Yuvi's in the 20-20. In spite of his generous tax moves and expenditure increases he has managed a fiscal deficit of only 2.5 per cent of GDP for next year, well below the 3 per cent mandated by the FRBM law. And while he is bringing down your favourite fiscal deficit, he is still successfully boosting overall demand through his expenditure hikes, excise cuts and income tax slab concessions. Quite a rope trick.

CE: You could say that. It's too good to be true. First off, if he really succeeds in bringing the fiscal deficit down from 3.1 per cent of GDP to 2.5 per cent, then he would have reduced the fiscal stimulus in the economy. It's the net position that counts, not every individual tax break or expenditure increase. But I don't think he will achieve the target because of four big items. The Sixth Pay Commission award is almost certain to increase expenditures by at least half a per cent of GDP. The farmer loan waiver costs are unfunded, whether in cash or bonds. The projected subsidies for food and fertiliser look under-budgeted, not to mention the strong likelihood of higher off-budget accommodation to the oil companies. And the 17 per cent income tax revenue increase looks way too optimistic after the big bonanza through tax slab changes. So expect additional government borrowing and some upward pressure on interest rates later in the year. But, oddly enough, the higher fiscal stimulus may not be all bad in a year when the foreign trade gap may widen and domestic consumption soften because of negative wealth effects.

GC: That's quite a concession from a fiscal fundamentalist like you. Sure you are feeling ok? Now I suppose you want to talk about the expenditure side. And I bet you only want to talk about the farm loan waiver. You guys don't care when overdues from rich industrialists are written off by banks. But you yell and scream about "moral hazard" and "credit culture" when poor farmers are given a break. Hey, did you see that Surjit Bhalla and Sunil Jain (*Business Standard*, 11 March) have estimated the waiver to be less than half FM's figure of Rs. 50,000 crore. So what's your problem?

CE: The loan waiver does bother me. It's not so much the fiscal burden, whatever that turns out to be. The real problem is that it conveys a powerful signal, which will undercut the initiatives for financial inclusion. Just think what this move does for the future climate for sound credit systems and subsidy containment when famous reformers like Manmohan Singh and Chidambaram are seen to be blessing *government*-sponsored loan waivers (that's very different from an individual bank writing off a particular industrialist's non-performing loan). We live in a populist democracy in populist times.

This move will encourage more competitive populism and undermine sound economic policies. As for all the other expenditure increases, they are not much different from previous budgets. The disappointment is that FM's earlier clarion call for more focus on "outcomes than on outlays" seems to ring a bit hollow after five UPA budgets.

GC: At least, you will admit that his revision of the income tax slabs after 10 years is both good politics and good economics? And the reduction in the CST to 2 per cent and the CENVAT rate to 14 per cent are moves in the right direction towards an integrated GST. Or are you going to carp about the tax proposals too?

CE: Well, you expect me to carp...so here goes. The tax slab revisions are good, though it would have been better if these were revised approximately in line with inflation every three years or so. I would have welcomed the CENVAT reduction more if the government had shown the courage to raise the general service tax rate closer to 14 per cent from the present 12. (By the way, how come legal services continue to escape inclusion under this tax?) And was it really necessary to continue tinkering with excise and customs duty rates on particular commodities? But my real unhappiness is with FM's continued proclivity to introduce odd new taxes. This time we have the CTT on futures trading in commodities and the effective hike in the rate of STT for stock traders. Both show an unfortunate affection for turnover taxes when the thrust of tax reform is towards taxing value added. The CTT could seriously hurt the nascent activity of commodity futures trading on organised exchanges. And the revision of the STT will hurt the brokerage business at a time when it's already reeling from massive declines in stock trading volume. But then neither group has political clout.

GC: You economists are complete bores, *yaar*. You are always looking for dark clouds when the sun is shining. Luckily, nobody cares what you think or write. Hey, how come you are titling this 'Year of the Carp' when everybody knows it's the Year of the Rat?

CE: Now look who's carping....

Business Standard, March 13, 2008.

23 Oil Bonds are no Solution

Oil bonds were invented more than a decade ago during the tenure of the United Front government when the present finance minister was serving in the same post. Arguably, they might have been a clever way of keeping rising petroleum subsidies off the government's budget books during a *temporary* spurt in world oil prices. What is becoming increasingly clear is that they are an opaque and hugely inadequate response to the current problem of *sustained* increases (over the last five years) in global oil prices. Let us understand why and look at some alternatives.

To begin with the obvious, the need for oil bonds, or any kind of subsidy, arises only because of the government's policy of keeping the consumer price of key distillates (diesel, petrol, kerosene, and LPG cylinders) fixed over long periods of time in the face of rising international prices of oil. The tortuous process of dismantling the decades old regime of the administered price mechanism (APM) in petroleum products came tantalisingly close to success during the NDA government. But it didn't quite make it and the successor UPA government has firmly entrenched the system of price controls and subsidies. Once price controls are imposed, the issue of subsidies follows naturally. The only questions relate to their precise form and content.

The lure of oil bonds as the preferred form of subsidy is twofold. First, and most importantly, in our system of cash-based government budgeting (and with no obligation to publish a government balance sheet) the transfer of oil bonds to the government-controlled oil marketing companies (OMCs: IOC, HPCL and BPCL) can be kept off the budget. It does not affect the fiscal and revenue deficits of the Central government at the time of transfer. This is a great advantage, especially when fiscal responsibility laws mandate specified targets for such deficits. Secondly, the cash impact of the bonds, in the form of interest payments to the holders and final repayment, is postponed and attenuated over time. From the viewpoint of the OMCs, of course, these features of oil bonds are huge negatives. They can't use petro bonds to buy oil or defray operational expenses. The flow of interest earnings is a trickle in relation to needs and only cumulates over time. Attempts to sell the bonds for cash typically result in large discounts, that is, when they are allowed to be traded at all.

The economic consequences of petro bonds are very similar to the obvious alternative of transparent cash subsidies from government to OMCs. In the latter case, government savings would fall (widening revenue deficit) and government borrowing requirements would increase (because of a higher fiscal deficit), with attendant upward pressures on interest rates and "crowding out" of private investment. In the oil bond case the OMCs take the hit in their profits, leading to lower taxes, lower retained earnings and lower distributed profits (to government), thus, reducing public savings in all three ways. And with less ready cash, the OMCs are driven to higher borrowings to meet their operational and investment expenses, resulting in similar upward pressure on interest rates in the economy.

To rub salt into the wound, the government is not even transferring oil bonds equivalent to the full amount of the OMCs' "under-recoveries" (a euphemism for their price-control-caused losses). According to reports of the latest government decision relating to OMC under-recoveries in 2007/08 (fixed at 70,000 crores by government), only half will be compensated by government through oil bonds, a third will be extracted from the profits of the producing companies (ONGC, OIL and GAIL), and the remaining 17 per cent will be "borne" by the OMCs (that is, they won't be compensated at all!). Notice, OMCs receive their dubious oil bonds in a very tardy manner: the end-February government budget owned up to only Rs. 11,257 crores of petro bond transfers, whereas the recently determined amount due for 2007/08 by the 50 per cent formula is Rs. 35,000 crores (not clear by when the remainder of this total will be transferred).

Another major anomaly of the present system is that the burden of oil subsidies falls almost exclusively on the government-controlled marketing and producing companies. The private refiners (such as Reliance and Essar) are raking in revenues exporting their products at soaring world prices. As one astute observer pointed out, what is happening is a *de facto* privatisation of the Indian oil and gas industry, with government companies being ground down by mounting losses and private ones thriving. Whether this result is occurring by accident or design is a moot question.

With world oil prices at $125/bbl (and possibly headed north) and our consumer prices calibrated at below $60/bbl (for break even), it is painfully obvious that the system is unsustainable. "Under-recoveries" in 2008/09 are estimated to range between Rs. 150,000 to 200,000 crores! It is not just the viability of our oil and gas *navaratnas* that is at stake. The OMCs are finding it increasingly difficult to fund their operations. Talk of *de facto* rationing of diesel and LPG has already hit the headlines. Very soon the government will find itself squeezed between the rock of having to raise prices and the hard place of rationing/queues/black markets.

What are the alternatives to the present disintegrating system? Basically, as this newspaper has lucidly pointed out in its editorial (May 16, 2008), we need two things: a much more transparent and operationally viable system of subsidy (for as long as it is required), and a calibrated path to raising petroleum product prices to increasingly reflect the hard facts of global scarcity. The switch to a transparent cash subsidy from government to OMCs can and should be accomplished swiftly. Yes, the deficit targets of the fiscal responsibility law will be breached by wide margins. But in the present environment the official deficit numbers simply hide huge repressed deficits without being able to mitigate their adverse economic consequences. Making the hidden deficits transparent may help generate more pressures for corrective action. Perhaps more importantly, the spectre of OMC-cash-shortage-driven disruptions to supply of oil products can be laid to rest.

As for price increases, only two things are obvious. You can't make a full price correction overnight. And you can't postpone the correction for ever. If, as seems likely, the world price of oil is likely to stay above $100/bbl for the foreseeable future, Indian producers and consumers have to adjust to that hard fact of life. Some targeted subsidies can be kept for a long time. For the rest, there really is no viable alternative to adjustment. Whether that adjustment is done over one, two or three years will depend much more on politics than economics. The longer it is postponed, the greater will be the economic damage.

Business Standard, May 22, 2008.

24 Subsidies to Perdition

Recent months have seen much concern and calls for action to contain the burgeoning subsidies for food, fertiliser, and fuel. For 2008/09 these subsidies are projected at 1, 2 and 3 (at least) per cent of GDP, respectively (see my last column in *Business Standard*, June 26). You could call it the "other" 1-2-3 agreement of the political executive! Actually, our penchant for subsidies is not a recent phenomenon. The habit is nearly six decades old and thrives despite pretty overwhelming evidence on its ruinous economic cost and general ineffectiveness. Just consider the following.

Electric Power: Subsidies for power have been a hardy perennial. Despite all kinds of executive and legislative efforts to minimise them, gross subsidies on electricity sales by state electricity boards rose to over Rs. 43,000 crores in 2007/08 or nearly one per cent of GDP. Over two-thirds is accounted for by sales to agriculture and the rest is for domestic use. And what has the long history of power subsidies got us other than financially parlous power utilities, weak state finances and over-priced supply to industry and commerce? Well, the other unfortunate results include: the tortuous history of guarantees and counter-guarantees (remember Enron-Dabhol?); perennial power deficits, including a record peak power deficit of 15 per cent in 2007/08; massive disruption to medium and small scale industry and commerce; over-use of groundwater and sinking water tables; and routine "load shedding" all over the country, including in the capital city of this "emerging economic superpower".

Irrigation: The second largest subsidy item in most state budgets is for irrigation water. Except for Gujarat and Maharashtra, water charges in irrigation schemes cover only a fraction of O&M costs, let alone the massive investments undertaken over decades in dams and canals. As a result, maintenance is poor and the irrigation potential of existing schemes is seriously under-utilised. Combined with sinking water tables, much of Indian agriculture is subject to water stress, leading to low productivity and weak growth. And, as we all know, these problems are hitting home this year through higher inflation.

Urban Water Supply: Under-pricing and subsidies are rampant here as well. Unlike in most of the world, Indian cities and towns are unable to supply water from the mains 24x7. Water and sanitation utilities are chronically under-financed, under-repaired and under-invested. The well-to-do invest in tanks and pumps to solve the supply problems and filter/boil to improve quality. Slum-dwellers are lucky if they can access piped sources and still suffer the health hazards of contamination. Many buy water from "informal" water-sellers at high prices. So, most of the subsidy goes to the rich and middle classes.

Fertilisers: Another hardy perennial in India's subsidy jungle, this one is borne by the Central budget and is mostly focused on urea. Despite the recommendations of a long and distinguished lineage of "High-Powered Committees", the price-control-cum-subsidy regime has persisted. So has the severe damage to soil quality from over-use of nitrates relative to potassium and phosphates. It has also discouraged new investment, with hardly any new capacity being created in the last 20 years. This leads to serious problems in periods of global scarcity, as at present.

Higher Education: Public universities and related institutions subsist on government subsidies, since absurdly low fees have not been revised in several decades. The predictable results have been inexorable decline in physical infrastructure and the quality of faculty. The problems are compounded by caste-based reservations. The rich have opted out of the system and send their youngsters to foreign universities (charging fees many multiples higher) or a small number of private, "non-profit" institutions. The less well-off have no option. Reform has been blocked by vested interests and misguided political leadership. Overall, the system is in crisis and bodes ill for India in this knowledge-based century.

Petroleum Products: The story of the huge oil subsidies needs no retelling. Aside from the massive damage to public sector oil companies and ballooning fiscal deficits, the price-subsidy structure is encouraging excessive "dieselization" of the economy, rampant adulteration of diesel with even cheaper kerosene (with resultant damage to the environment) and delayed adjustment to the inevitable.

Foodgrains: Arguably, the PDS-related food subsidy has had some successes, especially in its early years, in enhancing consumption and welfare of the urban poor. But, as the PDS administration has worsened over time (in step with the general administration), diversion, pilferage, mis-targeting and other forms of leakage have mounted. In any case, the distribution system only works moderately effectively in perhaps five states, which exclude the poorest and most populous, such as UP and Bihar.

There are many other examples. But the general point is clear enough. Some of India's worst performing sectors are those marked by the witches' brew of public supply, price controls and subsidies. It's impossible to think of a major sector with high subsidies which is performing well. In sharp contrast, just consider some of India's best performing sectors such as IT, telecom, pharmaceuticals, auto components, two-wheelers and entertainment (TV, films, etc.). None of these rely on subsidies. Most of the Indian manufacturing sector depended on "subsidies" of a different kind for several decades up to the early 1990s. High tariffs and import controls protected manufacturing units from cheaper imports and the Indian consumer paid the "subsidy" through inflated prices for domestic manufactures. As trade protection was gradually and systematically reduced throughout the next 15 years, these "subsidies" disappeared. Indian industry didn't collapse. On the contrary, it became much more efficient, resilient and dynamic. Again the lesson is clear: wean sectors off their subsidy crutches and they perform much better.

The different histories of two infrastructure sectors, power and telecom, is also instructive. The prolonged history of a subsidy culture (and virtual state monopoly over distribution) ensured the permanent semi-crisis in India's electric power sector. In contrast, the equally long-standing telecom public monopoly was not associated with a subsidy culture (except for a limited number of *netas* and *babus*). So, when the sector was opened up in the mid-1990s to private players and new mobile technologies, there was no burden of a subsidy culture blocking its progress. And we have all benefited from the astonishing growth and technical change ushered in by Indian entrepreneurs and companies in this key infrastructure sector.

The lesson is clear: subsidies (usually linked to public provision) pave the road to perdition. If we want to rescue India's poorly-performing sectors, we have to free up prices, phase out subsidies and allow free entry. It has worked before. It will work again.

Business Standard, July 10, 2008.

VI

Employment and Inequality

25 Rising Inequality?

Twice in the past week this paper has published cogent and thoughtful editorials on the subject of inequality in India (*Business Standard*, March 12 and 17), the first triggered by the publication of the latest Forbes list of global billionaires (with more Indian ones than Japanese!) and the second by the stark concurrence of record starting salary offers to IIM graduates and, rural distress and violence in Nandigram and Bijapur. The latter (a signed piece by Ninan) drew pointed attention to the "Dickensian paradox" of Rs. 10,000 *per day* starting pay being offered to management graduates while "farmers growing sugar, cotton and wheat struggle to make Rs. 10,000 in a whole cropping season". All is clearly not well in the state of India. Ninan concluded, "These are not coherent thoughts, but do we have a coherent state, and has this been a coherent week?" If he had waited a day, he could have thrown in the incoherent results of two simultaneous World Cup cricket matches in the West Indies, which made 1.3 billion South Asians deeply unhappy and another 150 million delirious with joy! This column reflects a search for coherence in my own thoughts on inequality in India.

Let's start with some numbers. As Table 25.1 shows, measured by standard indices of income and consumption inequality, such as the Gini index, India's distribution of consumption (we don't have a recently compiled, reliable survey of household income) compares favourably with most countries. (Remember, a lower Gini index means less inequality). Indeed, in the comparison with a sample of 16 other countries from all over the world, the only ones with a lower Gini than India are the two Scandanavian nations (Sweden and Norway), and the two richest East Asian countries, Japan and Korea. These four would actually have even lower Ginis if the comparison was with their consumption distributions and not the income distributions available in the WDI source. Even more interesting is the time trend of India's consumption Gini indices thrown up by successive large sample NSS surveys of consumer expenditure (on which official poverty estimates are based) since 1983. As Table 25.2 shows, this trend is almost as flat as a *chapati*, indicating

Table 25.1

Distribution of Income or Consumption for a Recent Year

		% Share of Income or Consumption	
	Gini Index	*Bottom 10%*	*Top 10%*
Brazil (2003)[b]	58.0	0.8	45.8
Chile (2000)[b]	57.1	1.2	47.0
China (2001)[a]	44.7	1.8	33.1
Egypt (1999/2000)[a]	34.4	3.7	29.5
France (1995)[b]	32.7	2.8	25.1
India (1999/2000)[a]	**32.5**	**3.9**	**28.5**
Indonesia (2002)[a]	34.3	3.6	28.5
Japan (1993)[b]	24.9	4.8	21.7
Korea (1998)[b]	31.6	2.9	22.5
Mexico (2002)[a]	49.5	1.6	39.4
Norway (2000)[b]	25.8	3.9	23.4
Philippines (2000)	46.1	2.2	36.3
Poland (2002)[a]	34.5	3.1	27.0
Russia (2002)[a]	39.9	2.4	30.6
Sweden (2000)[b]	25.0	3.6	22.2
UK (1999)[b]	36.0	2.1	28.5
US (2000)[b]	40.8	1.9	29.9

Note: a = Consumption; b = Income.

Source: World Development Indicators (2006).

Table 25.2

India: Gini Index of Consumption Distribution

1983	*1987/88*	*1993/94*	*1999/2000*	*2004/05*
30.3	30.2	30.1	32.0	32.1

Note: Consumption expenditure data collected on 30 days recall basis for food items and 365 days for selected non-food items.

Source: Surjit Bhalla, *Second Among Equals: The Middle Class Kingdoms of India and China*, IIE, 2007 (forthcoming); based on NSSO consumption surveys.

no serious worsening of inequality in measured consumption inequality during the quarter century of strong GDP growth since 1980.

All this is genuinely important data and probably carries a lot of persuasive reassurance in the well-appointed committee rooms of Yojana

Bhavan and North Block, and perhaps also in the even better furnished board rooms of India Inc.(though many incumbents of the latter might mistake a Gini for a new gin-based cocktail!). But it doesn't cut much ice with the millions of marginal farmers making around Rs. 10,000 a year when they hear that IIM graduates are offered over 300 times that amount as starting pay, or that entry level youngsters in BPOs pull in 20 times their annual earnings from back-breaking field labour. Nor does it assuage the envy and bitterness of the growing hordes of unemployed (and underemployed) with near worthless school–leaving certificates (or less) in the poor, populous states of the "cow belt", where economic opportunity and entrepreneurship are just big words with little reflection in their miserable realities. It doesn't even impress me when I see Rs. 80 lakh Mercedes sedans glide past the usual squalor of much of Delhi, with tinted windows firmly locked against the importuning of misshapen beggars at traffic lights. The inconvenient truth is that the visual prevalence of stark contrasts between the rich and the poor is on the rise in India. Such contrasts are heightened and deepened by the ongoing revolution in image-connectivity through TV, computers, mobile phones and other gizmos. They fan the political appeal of caste and class conflict, and populist responses.

Returning to less emotive terrain, let me summarise some basic facts. India's strong economic growth at an average rate of 6 per cent for the past 25 years (accelerating recently) has been a great boon for most of her citizens. The incidence of abject poverty has undoubtedly declined from nearly half of the population to less than a quarter. It wouldn't have happened without sustained growth. (So don't curb growth to promote equality!) History suggests that some rise in economic inequality is an inevitable concomitant of successful economic development as people shift from low-productivity, traditional agriculture to high productivity, modern industry, and services. At the same time, we should recognise that India's development could have been significantly more pro-poor. More importantly, it can be more pro-poor and egalitarian *in future* if we have the courage and political will to tackle four great weaknesses.

First, our policies must cease to discourage the rapid growth of employment-intensive manufacturing, which has been the key transmission mechanism for lifting people out of poverty in the past 100 years (or more) of global economic development. Where are the large-scale textile and garment factories in which school-leavers can look for decent blue-collar jobs? Mostly in China and other Asian countries; very few in India, thanks to our misguided labour laws, SSI reservations, and the terrible infrastructure of power, roads, water and ports. All these need correction through reform.

Second, our public education systems at all levels (primary, secondary and tertiary) have gone from bad to worse. Quantity and "throughput" may have increased but quality and skill-development (including literacy and numeracy) has fallen. In principle (and in practice in better run countries) decent public education offers the best hope for poorer segments to escape poverty and climb the ladder of opportunity. Inequality of economic outcomes may be inescapable. But greater equality in opportunity to avail good primary and secondary education can convert despair into hope. The policy agenda is enormous. All our policy-makers know what good schools are like (they send their children there), but they block the application of their organisational principles and practices in government schools. Such hypocrisy has to be surmounted.

Third, generalising from education, our Central and state governments have a poor record in building and sustaining the infrastructures of electric power, roads, water systems and other "quasi public goods". Their political masters have easily succumbed to the twin evils of subsidy-mongering and "jobs for the boys" overmanning. It is the lower deciles of the income pyramid that pay the heaviest penalty for malfunctioning public systems; the rich are adept at capturing subsidies and finding alternatives. The great lesson of the cellphone revolution is that the poor are willing to pay for services, when their quality is the same as for the rich.

Finally, there is the huge problem of entropy and decay in public administration of law and order. Order and security (and even "justice") can be bought by the rich, but certainly not by the poorest half of India's population. There is no quick fix here; so I won't pretend to offer one.

If India's future economic development is to be more egalitarian, these are some of the big issues that we need to grapple with. If they are beyond our collective reach, then take some solace from the tables in this column!

Business Standard, March 22, 2007.

26 Governance and Health

A fortnight ago India celebrated 60 years of Independence. There was much justifiable satisfaction expressed about the deep roots democracy has put down in Indian political soil over the last six decades. At the same time apprehensions were voiced about the declining standards of governance, not least during the extended debate over the election process for the President. On the economic front, the euphoria from four successive years of eight per cent plus growth and the booming asset markets were tempered by the rising tides of uncertainty in global finance and, more importantly, the growing appreciation of the dualities in India's economic performance: between an ever more confident and dynamic private sector and an increasingly sclerotic government sector; between the winners in the booming market economy and those left behind at its periphery; and between the rising remunerations of skilled labour and the many millions more of under-employed and uneducated youth, desperately seeking jobs and security.

Underlying these dualities is the massive under-performance in the provision of public services by all layers of government. Much has been written of the perennial inadequacies of public infrastructure (power, roads, water, sanitation, etc.) and the well-documented weaknesses in government education systems. There has been rather less discussion on the performance of our health sector. That is the focus of this piece, helped by the recently published National Family Health Survey 3 (NFHS-3) for 2005/06.

To begin with, how do India's key health parameters compare with other major developing countries, including our neighbours, China, Bangladesh, and Pakistan? The short answer is not well at all. On all the parameters in Table 26.1, India does substantially worse than China and Indonesia, let alone richer countries like Brazil, Mexico, Thailand, and Turkey. The World Health Organization (WHO) constructs an indicator of "Healthy Life Expectancy at birth" (HALE), which adjusts the normal life expectancy measure for years of serious illness/injury predicted from the data. By this measure, HALE for a girl baby in India in 2002 was only 54 years, compared to 65 in China, 68 in Mexico, and 71 in the US. On a direct measure of health service delivery,

Table 26.1

Some Key Indicators of Health

Country	*Gross National Income Per Capita (US$)*	*Life Expectancy at Birth (Years) Female*	*Healthy Life Expectancy (HALE) at Birth (Years) Female*	*Infant Mortality Rate (Per 1000 Live Births)*	*TB Prevalence (Per 1,00,000 Population)*	*Immunisation Coverage among One-year olds with three doses of DTP (%)*	*Children Aged < 5 Years Stunted for Age*	*Children Aged < 5 Years Underweight for Age*
	(2005)	*(2005)*	*(2002)*	*(2005)*	*(2005)*	*(2005)*		
Bangladesh	470	63	53	54	406	88	50.5 (2004)	42.7 (2004)
Brazil	3550	75	62	28	76	96	-	3.7 (2002-03)
China	1740	74	65	23	208	87	18.6 (2002)	6.1 (2002)
India	**730**	**64**	**54**	**56**	**299**	**59**	**38.4 (2005-06)** 1_/	**45.9 (2005-06)** 1_/
Indonesia	1280	69	59	28	262	70	28.6 (2004)	19.7 (2004)
Mexico	7310	77	68	22	27	98	15.5 (2006)	3.4 (2006)
Nigeria	560	48	42	101	536	25	43.0 (2003)	27.2 (2003)
Pakistan	690	62	52	80	297	72	41.5 (2001)	31.3 (2001)
Thailand	2720	73	62	18	204	98	15.5 (2006)	7.3 (2006)
Turkey	4750	74	63	26	44	90	19.1 (1998)	7.0 (1998)
US	43560	80	71	7	3	96	3.3 (1999-2002)	1.1 (1999-2002)

Note: 1_/ : From NFHS-3; relates to <3 years age category.

Source: World Health Statistics, 2007, WHO; GNI per capita from World Development Indicators (2007), World Bank.

immunisation coverage of one-year-olds for DTP, India scores particularly badly, even in comparison to Pakistan and Bangladesh. Perhaps most shocking, 46 per cent of young children in India are underweight for age, compared to 6 per cent in China, 20 per cent in Indonesia, 31 per cent in Pakistan, and 27 per cent in Nigeria.

Perhaps even more pertinent and interesting (or should I say disquieting?) are the trends in key health indicators, especially for children, in the last 15 years presented in Table 26.2. The time period with comparable data is relatively short because the NFHS survey series was only launched in 1992-1993. The data suggest that India's children (our future?) have been getting a very raw deal, with little progress in key indicators over the last 15 years of unusually strong economic growth. Indeed, if you compare 2005-06 to 1998-99, there is hardly any improvement at all. True, the proportion of children under 3 years who are "stunted" has come down. On the other hand, the proportion of children in that age group who are anaemic has *increased* from 74 to 79 per cent. So has the incidence of anaemia in married women. Sixty years after Independence, four out of five Indian children suffer from anaemia—surely a devastating commentary on our health and nutrition policies. The proportion of one-year-olds receiving three doses of DTP vaccine remained unchanged. So did the percentage of children with diarrhoea receiving oral rehydration salts, at a low 26 per cent. This suggests that the health delivery services at the grassroots level have not improved despite rising allocations of funds and manpower.

Table 26.2

Health of India's Children: Some Indicators

	NFHS – 3 (2005–06)	*NFHS – 2 (1998–99)*	*NFHS – 1 (1992–93)*
Children 12-23 months who have received 3 doses of DPT vaccine (%)	55.3	55.1	51.7
Children with diarrhoea in the last 2 weeks who received ORS (%)	26.2	26.9	17.8
Children with diarrhoea in the last 2 weeks taken to a health facility (%)	58.0	65.3	61.9
Children under 3 years who are stunted (%)	38.4	45.5	na
Children under 3 years who are underweight %)	45.9	47.0	51.5
Children age 6-35 months who are anaemic (%)	79.2	74.2	na
Ever-married women age 15-49 who are anaemic (%)	56.2	51.8	na

Source: *http://www.nfhsindia.org/factsheet.html*

Table 26.3

State of Health in States, 2005-06

Key Indicators	*Bihar*	*Uttar Pradesh*	*Madhya Pradesh*	*Gujarat*	*Maharashtra*	*West Bengal*	*Andhra Pradesh*	*Tamil Nadu*	*Kerala*
1. Infant Mortality Rate (per 1000 live births in the last 5 years)	62.0	73.0	70.0	50.0	38.0	48.0	53.0	31.0	15.0
2. Children 12-23 months who have received 3 doses of DPT vaccine (%)	46.1	30.0	49.8	61.4	76.1	71.5	61.4	95.7	84.0
3. Children with diarrhoea in the last 2 weeks who received ORS (%)	22.2	12.0	28.6	28.3	37.8	43.7	36.0	29.0	34.6
4. Children with diarrhoea in the last 2 weeks taken to a health facility (%)	48.7	55.9	60.1	59.8	77.8	52.7	61.4	60.1	67.4
5. Children under 3 years who are stunted (%)	42.3	46.0	39.9	42.4	37.9	33.0	33.9	25.1	21.1
6. Children under 3 years who are underweight (%)	58.4	47.3	60.3	47.4	39.7	43.5	36.5	33.2	28.8
7. Children age 6-35 months who are anaemic (%)	87.6	85.1	82.6	80.1	71.9	69.4	79.0	72.5	55.7
8. Ever-married women age 15-49 who are anaemic (%)	68.3	50.8	57.6	55.5	49.0	63.8	62.0	53.3	32.3

Source: *http://www.nfhsindia.org/factsheet.html*

India is a big and diverse nation, we were repeatedly reminded at the 60th anniversary. So it behooves us to look at health indicators across some Indian states. There are not too many surprises here (Table 26.3).

As expected, Bihar and UP define the bleak end of health parameters, while Kerala and Tamil Nadu provide the beacons of hope. Most people know this but it is worth reminding ourselves that the infant morality rate in UP is five times higher than in Kerala, and two and a half times higher than in Tamil Nadu. (Parenthetically, it is interesting to note that after nearly 30 years of CPM rule, 44 per cent of children under 3 years in West Bengal are underweight for age.) This enormous variation defines both the challenge and the potential for bringing about improvements in future. But they won't happen by themselves. It requires both sustained increases in income and employment in the lagging states and major upgrading of health service (including clean water supplies) delivery. And all this will largely depend on the policies and efforts at the level of the respective states. There are no magic wands that the Central government can wave, with the possible exception of loosening the current anti-employment labour laws.

So, as we celebrate 60 years of political independence and take pride in our dynamic private sector, our remarkable IT successes and all the other usual dimensions of success, let us remind ourselves that a great deal remains to be done to improve the foundations of India's human resources—the health and well-being of our hundreds of millions of children. Without reasonably good health, the prospects for learning and skill development are bleak...and without that, so is our long-term future as a thriving and prosperous nation.

Business Standard, August 30, 2007.

27 OECD on India's Labour Market

A few weeks ago the OECD published its first *Economic Survey* on India. After a day-long seminar at the Imperial hotel, followed by some desultory reporting in a few pink papers, the document seems to have been buried in dusty bookshelves without much fanfare or debate. This reception is at par with the current treatment of periodic reports on the Indian economy by other international agencies, such as the World Bank, the IMF, the Asian Development Bank and so forth, not to mention the avalanche of publications from invest banks and fund houses. Fifteen years ago, when the Indian economy was weaker and more vulnerable, such documents provoked lengthy and passionate discussion in the press and frequent parliament questions. Now, with 8-9 per cent economic growth a routine occurrence and a bulging portfolio of forex reserves, such reports provoke little interest and even less passion. What can the industrial countries tell us when we are buying up their steel plants and luxury car brands? That seems to be the implicit hubris.

Well, if we can extricate ourselves from this complacent, "know all" mentality for a moment, I would recommend Chapter 4 of the present volume for a thorough read. The rest of the report is a fairly competent but largely unexceptional review of the usual terrain: growth, infrastructure, fiscal balances, financial system, human capital and so on. They can be skipped. But Chapter 4 on India's labour market merits careful perusal. It not only provides an up-to-date and analytical treatment of the well-known issues but, more refreshingly, it offers new perspectives and fresh, survey-based analysis.

In the first category, it reminds us that although total employment growth in the five years to 2004/05 has averaged a healthy 2.9 per cent per annum and industrial employment has increased by over 6 per cent annually, organised industrial sector employment has been *declining* at about 1 per cent per year, bringing the share of organised industrial sector employment down from around 18 per cent (of total industrial employment) in 1998 to only 10 per cent in 2004. That is, over this period there has been increasing "casualization" of the industrial labour force. The OECD's diagnosis of the reasons for this trend is in line with conventional wisdom: "The bulk of the growth in employment has been created in very small enterprises. There is much evidence that the main reason for the lack of job creation in the 'organized' or formal part of the private sector is the restrictive legislation governing regular employment in larger firms."

There is much more along these lines, which is noteworthy but unremarkable. The novelty begins with the ranking of India's employment protection legislation (EPL) using the standard OECD methodology for assessing labour laws. The report finds that for *regular contracts*, "India's labour laws are stricter than those of all but two OECD countries, Portugal and the Czech Republic" (Panel A of Figure 27.1). Interestingly, China scores an EPL

Figure 27.1

International Comparison of Employment Protection Legislation in 2006

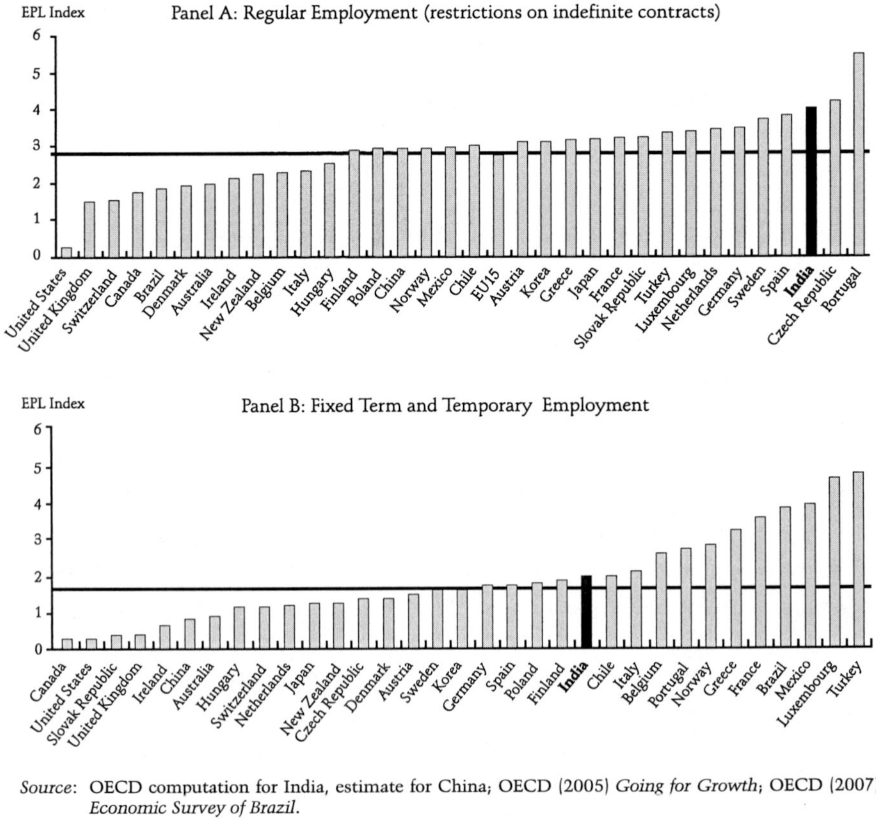

Source: OECD computation for India, estimate for China; OECD (2005) *Going for Growth*; OECD (2007) *Economic Survey of Brazil*.

index of close to the OECD average. Furthermore, if the notorious Chapter VB of the Industrial Disputes Act (which requires prior government permission for laying off employees in factories with more than 100 workers) "were not in force, the EPL for regular contracts would fall to the OECD average." For *collective dismissals*, India's EPL score is even worse, the strictest for all countries in the comparison and close to the maximum score of 6 on the EPL index.

Turning to fixed term and temporary employment, the OECD methodology finds India's EPL regime "more relaxed...placing it just above the mean of OECD countries" (Panel B of Figure 27.1). This moderation of EPL strictness is mainly because of allowing employees to work on temporary work agency contracts to carry on a range of "non-core" activities. However, it is noteworthy that even in this area India's EPL score is at least double of China's. Unsurprisingly, the report finds that net employment of *contractual* staff rose by 9 per cent a year between 1998 and 2004 in industrial units (covered by Annual Surveys of Industry), while employment declined by 2 per cent per year for *regular* workers. Moreover, again as expected, net job growth was a healthy 16 per cent per year in small (less than 100 workers) ASI units and a *negative* 5.5 per cent in large (more than 100 workers) ASI enterprises.

The consequences of strict EPL for regular workers in large industrial enterprises have been rising capital intensity (in a labour surplus economy!) and falling share of wages in value added. Furthermore, as Figure 27.2 shows and the report notes, the onerous burden of labour laws and other regulations encourage businesses to "start small and stay small. As a consequence, the size distribution of businesses in India is highly skewed towards small units with visible peaks in the distribution of plant sizes at 10 and 20 workers" (corresponding to the definitional cut-off for organised *versus* informal sector, with and without power). "Such small production reduces the efficiency of the economy and limits the productivity and incomes of businesses and workers."

Moving on, the OECD report breaks fresh ground by constructing a new, survey-based index of *state-level* reforms of labour laws and procedures in eight specific areas: the Industrial Disputes Act, the Factories Act, the Shops and Commercial Establishments Act, the Contract Labour Act, the role of inspectors, the maintenance of registers, the filing of returns and union representation. The index aims to "reflect the extent to which procedural changes have reduced transaction costs, through limiting the scope of regulations, providing greater clarity in their application, or simplifying compliance procedures." Based on

Figure 27.2

Plant Size Distribution in the Organised Manufacturing Sector by Size of Employment

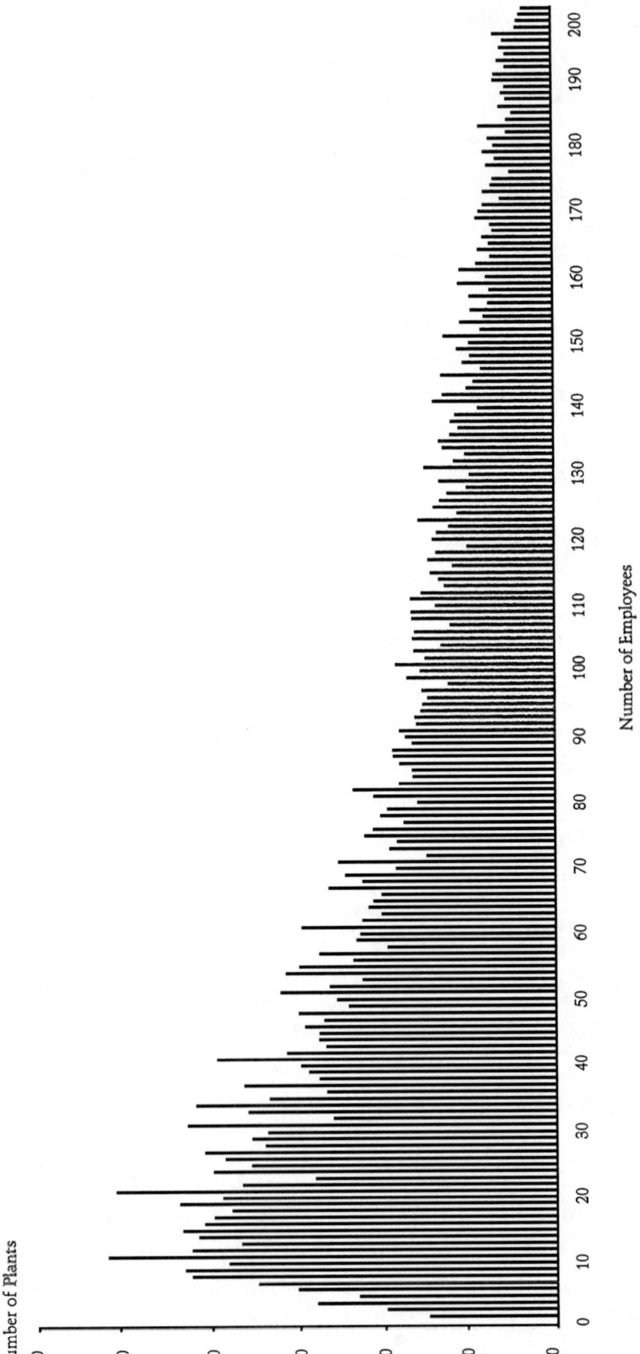

Note: Sizes rounded to the nearest even number.

Source: OECD calculation from ASI plant level data.

the index and some cross-state statistical analyses, the report offers some interesting results.

First, there is enormous variation across India's states in the extent of EPL reforms in recent years. Thus, Gujarat, UP, and Andhra Pradesh have done significant reforms, whereas Chhattisgarh, Goa, and Bihar have done very little. Second, there is reasonable correlation between the reform index and job turnover rates in industry, "suggesting that states that have made more reforms to their labour rules and regulations indeed obtain more flexibility (in terms of job dynamics) in their labour markets and vice- versa." Third, across the states in the period 2000 to 2004, the data suggests that an increase in job turnover rates has limited the fall in the labour share of value added. Fourth, higher rates of organised sector job creation appear to damp the rise in the size of the informal sector employment.

Well, I hope I have whetted your appetite for reading the full chapter of this OECD report.

Business Standard, January 10, 2008.

28 A Billion Peons Now?

Last week there was a front page news item in a national daily (*Indian Express*, 17 April), which caught my eye. It reported that over 11,000 applicants had applied for the posts of three (yes, three) peons advertised by the Haryana Electricity Regulatory Commission (HERC). The interviews under way are "likely to continue for three months and certain commission members and officers are working on this full-time." To me the report exemplified some of the key failures of our economic and social policies.

First, and most obviously, there is clearly something hugely wrong with our employment policies and outcomes. Some years ago I had questioned the hype about India's long-term potential attributed to the "demographic dividend" of a young and rapidly increasing labour force (*Business Standard*, November 25, 2003). As I had pointed out, this potential dividend refers to the supply of labour. The realisation of the potential for higher employment and output depends crucially on following appropriate policies for stimulating the *demand* for labour. The massive mismatch between supply and demand indicated by the *Express* report clearly suggests that our policies have fallen well short of ideal. It is particularly disquieting given that the event is occurring in one of our richest states and *after* the Indian economy has recorded an unprecedented five years of economic growth averaging over 8.5 per cent a year.

The second problem illustrated by this huge supply-demand mismatch relates to our education system. In the domain of public sector jobs in India, the minimum qualifications specified for a peon's position are among the lowest. So, what the mismatch tells me is that after 60 years of Independence our education system (mostly public) is doing a pretty poor job. This is well documented by numerous government and non-government reports and studies. According to official data, over one-third of school students drop out by Standard V and the rate climbs to almost 60 per cent by Standard VIII. What's more, as the extremely informative annual surveys by Pratham show, the literacy and numeracy skills attained in schools (especially government ones) are quite low. Serious problems plague not just our schools. They extend to vocational training institutes, colleges and most institutions of higher learning. The net result is that our education system produces hundreds of millions of people with low skills. The over supply of candidates for posts of peons is very sad but perhaps unsurprising.

The enormous labour market mismatch in this vignette is, of course, amplified by the distorted wage policy followed by Central and state governments. Under this policy the executive cadres of the government salariat (including the IAS, IFS, IPS, etc., which media comments usually focus on) are typically underpaid relative to comparators in the private sector, while the bottom rungs (including peons) are generally paid much more (about twice as much according to some studies) than their private sector counterparts. Quite apart from the large fiscal implications (since the lower ranks account for over 95 per cent of government employees), this leads to other distortions in the labour market. For example, a private primary school teacher usually earns much less than a government peon. Such distortions will be magnified when the recommendations of the Sixth Pay Commission are implemented.

Fourth, the report highlights the dysfunctional nature of many governmental bodies, thanks to the onerous burden of recruitment (and other) rules under which they labour. If several HERC members and other officers are going to spend three months full-time to interview the 11,000 plus candidates, surely their mandated responsibility of electricity regulation will suffer grievously. The primacy of rules and procedures over common sense and efficiency is quite remarkable. No serious private sector organisation would follow such a tortuous and enormously costly procedure to fill three posts of peons. That's mainly because the efficiency of their operations is subject to the market discipline of the "bottom line". In government organisations, accountability is defined principally in terms of rules and procedures, not in terms of efficiency, profit or service standards. Of course, as we all know, rules and procedures are often bent or side-stepped to accommodate graft and corruption, but that's all done "under the table", not on the record. To me this massive misallocation of HERC's resources of senior manpower to cull out three peons out of 11806 applicants exemplifies much that is wrong with the day to day functioning of our public sector.

Finally, returning to the first point, the huge mismatch simply reflects the enormous scarcity of decent jobs with some security (probably excessive in this instance) for those with low education and skill levels. The Indian economy has undoubtedly enjoyed good growth for a quarter of century, with remarkable acceleration in the last five years. In aggregate terms growth has even been "job-full". The National Sample Survey (61st Round) data show that employment increased by a healthy 2.9 per cent per year between 1999/2000 and 2004/05. But the fact is that the overwhelming preponderance of this employment expansion has been in the informal sector, where earnings are low and job security even lower. Rapid growth of labour-intensive manufacturing, that great development machine for creating decent low-skill jobs in poor countries, has run into all sorts of obstacles in India, including anti-employment labour laws, bad infrastructure, small-scale industry reservation policies, and (until a few years ago) distorted foreign trade policies. Most recently, there has been the added burden of an appreciating currency, much favoured by the finance boys (and girls).

There are some who believe that India can successfully pursue a development strategy which skips the stage where labour-intensive manufacturing plays a dominant role in the economy. They point to the recent successes of "modern" services sectors such as information technology, BPO, KPO, telecom, media, and so forth. Well, may be. I just want to know how many of the 11803 disappointed candidates of the HERC peon recruitment process can reasonably aspire to jobs in these sectors, given the limited qualifications they have. The answer to that question could have much to do with the future of India.

Business Standard, April 24, 2008.

VII

GENERAL

29 Only One New Giant for Now?

Last week I was in Beijing for yet another conference on the rise of Asia (especially China and India) and its implications for the global economy. Before turning to substance, let me share a few casual impressions about China's capital city, which I was revisiting after 15 years. Beijing was cold, spacious, orderly and confidently prosperous: smooth wide roads and pavements, plenty of new cars and buses (but very few bicycles and no motorised two-wheelers), throngs of warmly (often fashionably) clad and well-shod pedestrians in the streets and shopping malls, lots of new commercial centres and residential blocks laid out in a planned urban development format and impressive highways (with giant cloverleaf crossings) ringing the city. It reminded me much more of well-planned, industrial country cities like Hamburg and Nagoya (which have been almost wholly rebuilt after the destruction of WWII) than of any infrastructure-starved, (often) chaotic, slum-scarred Indian metropolis. On return, the contrast with Delhi's dingy little "international" airport, with its anarchic parking lot and blanket-huddled taxi drivers, was quite stark. Official data say that average income in China is approximately double of India's. Visual appearances suggest that Beijing is at least thrice as rich as Delhi and much better organised.

At the conference I had been asked to talk about India's growth and its implications for the world economy. Here is the gist of what I said, with the focus on the implications. India's growth at an average rate of almost 6 per cent a year over the past quarter of a century (with per capita growth of nearly 4 per cent a year) is both remarkable and commendable. Certainly, back in 1980, there was almost no respectable scholar or institution predicting such sustained development of this poverty-ridden, populous country. At the same time, the prevailing fashion of bracketing India's rise with China's exceptionally dynamic development under rubrics like "China and India Rising" or "Dancing with Giants" may mask more than it reveals. If India's development in the last 25 years has been good, China's has been extraordinary. Furthermore, while India has been a gradual "globaliser", China's surging development has been far more intensively based on global trade and capital flows.

As a consequence, the global economic impact of China's rise has been much more dramatic in terms of the usual metrics of international economic relations: trade, capital flows and energy. What's more, China's integration with the world economy has accelerated sharply in recent years, especially after her entry into WTO in 2001. A glance at Table 29.1 illustrates this. The comparison of columns 5 and 6 is particularly instructive. It highlights both the dramatic increase in China's engagement with the world economy over the five years 2000 to 2005, as well as the much milder rise in India's international economic integration. For example, China's goods exports *increased* by an amount which was five times India's *total* goods exports in 2005. During these scant five years, China's share of world exports jumped from 3.9 to 7.3 per cent, while India's share rose sedately from 0.7 to 0.9 per cent. The *increment* in inward FDI flows into China was seven times total FDI inflows into India

Table 29.1

China and India: Global Impact

	China		*India*		*Increment (2000-2005)*	
	2000 *(1)*	*2005* *(2)*	*2000* *(3)*	*2005* *(4)*	*China* *(5)*	*India* *(6)*
Merchandise Exports ($ billion)[a,b]	249.1	762.4	45.5*	104.7*	513.3	59.2
Share of World Exports (%)[e]	3.9	7.3	0.7	0.9	3.4	0.2
Service Exports ($ billion)[a,b]	30.4	74.4	16.2*	60.6*	44	44.4
Current Account Balance ($ billion)[a,b]	20.5	160.8	-2.7*	-10.6*	140.3	-7.6
Foreign Exchange Reserves ($ billion)[a]	165.6	818.9	37.2	131.0	653.3	93.8
FDI Inflow ($ billion)[c]	30.1#	72.4	1.7#	6.6	42.3	4.9
FDI Stock (Inward, $ billion)[c]	193.3	317.9	17.5	45.3	124.6	27.8
Oil Consumption (million tonnes)[d]	223.6	327.3	106.1	115.7	103.7	9.6
Primary Energy Consumption (million tonnes oil equivalent)[d]	966.7	1554.0	320.4	387.3	587.3	66.9

Note: * Data for India refer to fiscal year 2000-01 and 2005-06.
1990-2000 (Annual Average).

Sources: a *International Financial Statistics*, December 2006 (*http://ifs.apdi.net/imf/*)
b RBI, *Handbook of Statistics on the Indian Economy*, 2005/06 (*www.rbi.org.in*)
c UNCTAD, *World Investment Report* , 2006 (*www.unctad.org*)
d *Statistical Review of World Energy*, 2006 (*http://www.bp.com/statisticalreview*)
e *International Trade Statistics*, 2001 and 2005 (*http://www.wto.org/english/res_e/statis_e/statis_e.htm*)

in 2005. Similarly, the *increase* in oil consumption in China was almost equal to India's *total* oil consumption in 2005.

Aside from the dominant factor of China's full-blooded embrace of global opportunities (compared to the much more hesitant policy stances adopted by India) there are several other reasons which explain these strikingly different outcomes. First, over the last 25 years, China's per capita growth rate has been about double of India's, around 8 per cent as compared to 4 per cent. So, depending on how you measure it, today China's economy is perhaps two and a half times as large as India's. Second, India's growth has been propelled more by domestic consumption than external demand as compared to China. Third, China's growth has been powered much more by the rapid growth of industry, especially labour-intensive manufactured exports, while in India the growth of services (mostly non-tradeables) has been more dominant. (It is a striking fact that the share of manufacturing in GDP in 2004 was only 16 per cent in India as compared to nearly 40 per cent in China.)

Even in services, China's total services exports exceeded India's in 2005 and the increment over 2000 was comparable in absolute terms, though the rate of growth was lower. The one area where India has displayed China type growth rates is software exports, which quadrupled from about $6 billion in 2000/01 to $24 billion in 2005/06. But even in 2005/06 (and despite all the media coverage and hype) the IT/ITES sub-sector accounted for less than 3 per cent of India's GDP and employed (according to NASSCOM) about 1.3 million workers directly (and perhaps double that number indirectly). By itself this sector cannot be expected to transform India's economy and employment profile. Although the potential for software export growth remains high, the pace of expansion has moderated as skill shortages have increased, competitors have risen and anti-"outsourcing" sentiments have hardened in importing nations.

The thrust of these remarks is that India's economic rise poses few adjustment problems for the rest of the world. That has certainly been the experience so far (with the limited exception of software exports). It is only fair to acknowledge an alternative view, which perceives India's development as simply lagging China's by 10 to 15 years, suggesting that by then India's economic engagement with the global economy will rival China's today. On balance, I don't think so. The medium-term future is more likely to resemble the past decade's experience. Barring unforeseen political or economic turmoil, in the next 10 years the global economy will have to contend with only one new burgeoning "giant", as it already has in the decade past. India's economic rise in global commerce, capital and energy transactions is likely to remain gradual and (hopefully) sustained. In 20 years, it may be a different story.

Business Standard, January 25, 2007.

30 The UPA's Economic Legacy

If you were an early migratory bird flying over the nation's capital last month on your way to winter in the Bharatpur sanctuary, you might have looked down and been deeply distressed by the plight of some of your feathered friends, notably the "lame ducks" and "headless chickens" limping/running around Delhi. I will withhold any comment on the latter category lest I trespass on the well recognised authority of my former *sarkari* colleague, Ronen Sen, who is reported to have expounded on the species in some important committees recently. Actually, I won't have all that much to say about lame ducks either. Numerous publications have already noted the lame duck nature of the Gandhi-Singh led UPA government, ever since each of the duo publicly announced, in mid-October, their retreat from a political showdown with the Left on the US nuclear deal. The only issue is whether the life of the limping government will extend to spring 2008 or 2009. Most of the betting seems to be on the former. In which case, it may not be too premature to attempt a preliminary assessment of the economic legacy of four years of UPA government, from spring 2004 to spring 2008 (while making some assumptions for the remaining few months of the period).

To begin with the obvious, these last four years have witnessed remarkable buoyancy of the economy. Economic growth has averaged an awesome 8.5 per cent, well above the standard 6 per cent being predicted by most analysts (including myself) at the beginning of the period. Aggregate savings and investment have risen from around 27-28 per cent of GDP to about 34-35 per cent. Exports of both goods and services have grown rapidly, at least until mid-2007. Net foreign capital inflows have soared from about $17 billion in 2003/04 to perhaps four times that level in 2007/08. Surging capital inflows and booming corporate profits helped triple stock market valuations between spring 2004 and November 2007. Forex reserves more than doubled during this period to exceed $270 billion by November 2007. Despite record economic growth and booming asset markets, inflation has been mostly contained within a 4 to 6 per cent range. We don't yet know the fallout for poverty and employment, since the most recent large sample NSS surveys were conducted in 2004/05.

This unprecedented economic boom has coincided with UPA's tenure. But was it caused or strengthened by the government's economic policies? The majority of non-official analysts (including this one) would attribute the remarkable dynamism to other factors, including: the cumulative impact of economic reforms since 1991; the buoyant world economy and burgeoning flows across borders of commerce, finance and technology (globalisation in short); the rising middle class, fuelling higher consumption and savings; the demographic dividend of a young population; the maturing of a strong and efficient private corporate sector; the spread of the IT/telecom revolution; and so forth. In two areas, government policies played important growth-supporting roles: the modest but significant decline in the consolidated fiscal deficit from 8.5 per cent of GDP in 2003/04 to 6.4 per cent in 2006/07; and (until spring 2007) the well calibrated monetary and exchange rate policies conducted by the RBI.

In assessing the UPA's legacy the more pertinent question might be: have the government's policies in these four years strengthened the sustainability of the recent growth spurt and enhanced its "inclusiveness"? The answer is not favourable. Just look at the record. Infrastructure remains a serious bottleneck, especially in electric power (peak deficits are at record levels), urban infrastructure, water supply (both urban and rural) and roads. The promise of the Electricity Act (2003) remains largely unfulfilled. The flagship National Highway Development Programme of the NDA government has quite clearly lost momentum in recent years. And most state roads remain atrocious. Perhaps most worrying has been the government's ostrich-like approach to the massive increase in global oil prices. With domestic oil prices controlled and largely static, subsidies to oil consumers (mostly well-off) have soared and domestic oil companies have been severely weakened. Indeed, the worst features of the old administered price mechanism (APM) have been resurrected.

In the financial world, pension reforms remain stalled and the growth of insurance continues to be constrained by stringent limits on foreign ownership. More importantly, banking remains hobbled by the dominance of government-owned banks and the UPA government's proclivity for proliferating interest rate controls.

The UPA's efforts to enhance the inclusiveness of economic growth have been stunted by the government's failure to reform the anti-employment labour laws that have throttled the expansion of formal sector employment in India for decades, especially since the mid-1970s. Decent job opportunities for the burgeoning supply of unskilled and low-skilled labour (the labour force already exceeds 450 million) continue to be limited and discouraged by unreformed labour laws. This leaves many millions trapped in casual jobs or low-productivity agriculture. The government's efforts to improve inclusiveness have focused on higher spending on a wide range of social and anti-poverty programmes. Unfortunately, almost all of them suffer from grievously deficient delivery systems because of inefficiency, corruption and lack of effective accountability. Indeed, there is widespread belief that the problems of misgovernance and corruption, have increased in recent years, as have the disparities between regions, urban-rural, formal-informal, and rich-poor. Looking ahead in the medium-term, this legacy is particularly damaging for education, health and rural infrastructure services, rendering the goal of "inclusive growth" rather distant. In the crucial sector of education, the government's preoccupation with caste-based reservation policies and maintenance of control over elite institutions of higher education have detracted from meaningful and urgently required reforms.

Even the government's relatively successful macroeconomic policies are at risk. The modest progress with fiscal consolidation is increasingly threatened by the rapid increase in off-budget subsidies for petroleum products, fertilisers and food, which may amount to nearly 2 per cent of GDP. The Sixth Pay Commission report, due in 2008, is very likely to entail a significant additional fiscal burden (was it really necessary to set it up last year?). Populist spending, already growing fast, is bound to accelerate between now and the general elections. Since spring 2007, the management of the exchange rate has faltered, permitting undue rupee appreciation to take a rising toll of growth in tradable goods and services.

For all these reasons the UPA's legacy for sustaining rapid and inclusive economic growth in future leaves a lot to be desired. It surely could have been far better.

Business Standard, November 22, 2007.

31 Conference Titbits

The Delhi conference season is in full swing. It's not just high-profile, business events organised by WEF, CII, FICCI, etc. Academic conferences, sponsored by think tanks and foundations, are also in full bloom. Last week there were back-to-back ones on a couple of hardy perennials: "Capital Flows" and "India, China in the Global Economy". Let me share a few interesting titbits from the varied menu on offer.

Barry Eichengreen (of Berkeley) presented a thoughtful paper in which he outlined four very different schools of thought on free capital flows across borders to developing countries: first, the textbook case for free capital movements in search of efficient capital allocation; second, an advocacy of free flows based on foreign capital as a vehicle for technology, modern management and pressures for institutional reform in the host country; third, a cautionary tale associating capital account liberalisation with instability and financial crises, and emphasising the critical importance of sequencing reforms; and finally, the challenges posed by capital surge and the associated problems of real exchange rate appreciation.

It's interesting to note how mainstream academic views in the West have matured over the last decade. Back in the mid-1990s (and despite the "tequila crisis" of 1993/94) the US Treasury and the IMF were leading the charge in favour of rapid implementation of capital account convertibility (CAC) in developing nations, including through espousal of enabling amendments of the IMF's Articles of Agreement. At that time one didn't hear too much about the latter two schools of thought in Eichengreen's list. The Asian financial crisis of 1997/98 and the Russian debt default of 1998 provided a couple of hard knocks in the school of experience. More recently, the astonishing rise of China and the recent spurt in India's economic growth (both without the benefits of CAC) have contributed to muting the demands for CAC implementation in developing nations.

It is now both more commonplace and reassuring to find mainstream Western economists emphasising the importance of prior conditions (fiscal consolidation, banking reform and mature financial regulation) to CAC and appreciating the relevance and suitability of "intermediate" exchange rate regimes for poor, labour-surplus developing countries. Thus, Eichengreen is comfortable with the view that "it is more prudent that capital account liberalization wait on the prior implementation of other reforms to avoid precipitating a crisis". He also seems to applaud China's policy of maintaining partial capital controls and taking recourse to "sterilized" foreign exchange intervention to maintain a competitive real exchange rate policy aimed at nurturing rapid, labour-intensive growth. Presumably, by extension of the same logic, he would bless similar policies in India.

Barry Bosworth (of Brookings) and co-authors presented an account of the US trade with China and India. Their paper is rich in analysis and data. I will limit myself to a couple of points. First, as Table 31.1 shows, the US has a huge imbalance (net deficit) in its goods trade with China and a more modest one in its trade with India. The table also brings out the smallness of India's goods trade with the US in comparison to China. In the authors' words, "India represents a sharp contrast to China in the small size of its goods trade. Although India's GDP is a third that of China's, its global trade is only about 12 per cent as large while its trade with the United States is less than 10 per cent as large."

Table 31.1

Trade with China and India, 2005

(billions of US dollars)

Bilateral US Trade with:		*Goods*	*Services*
China	Exports	58.2	13.4
	Imports	269.1	12.1
	Balance	-211.0	1.4
India	Exports	8.0	5.2
	Imports	19.9	5.0
	Balance	-11.9	0.1
Global Trade			
China	Exports	1054.5	146.8
	Imports	930.8	119.4
	Balance	123.8	27.4
India	Exports	102.2	55.8
	Imports	134.7	48.0
	Balance	-32.5	7.8

Source: As cited in Bosworth *et al.* (2007): IMF Directions of Trade Statistics for goods trade and OECD for services trade.

More surprising are Bosworth's finding that "China's global trade in services is substantially larger than India's"....and that "the United States reports a larger volume of services trade with China than India" despite all the hoopla about outsourcing of US service jobs to India. Digging deeper, Bosworth notes that in "recent years India has consistently reported a level of exports to the US of Business, Professional and Technical (BPT) Services that is twenty times that recorded by the United States as an import—$8,700 million in 2003 *versus* $402 million, for example, in 2003." This is an astonishingly huge discrepancy. According to Bosworth, most of it is attributable to accounting quirks on the Indian side, notably the inclusion of earnings of Indian software workers residing in the US (even if they intend to stay more than a year) and the inclusion of "internal sales of services to local affiliates of US firms as part of its exports". These definitional differences in the concepts of service exports are massive. Surely RBI and/or government need to bring out a lucid explanation of these differences and their implications for the economic analysis of India's service exports.

Turning to the third and last titbit, Alan Heston (of Pennsylvania) explored the puzzles that arise when he tried to reconcile the national GDP growth rate estimates of China and India with those thrown up by the purchasing-power-parity (PPP) estimates of GDP constructed by the long-running International Comparisons Project (ICP), which are reported in the Penn World Tables (PWT). (By the way, Heston is a co-progenitor of this 40-year old enterprise of producing GDP estimates for countries based on internationally comparable prices.) Specifically, the big puzzle is that if the PWT data are accepted at face value then the ratio of India's per capita GDP to China's (PPP-adjusted) is a plausible 0.6 in 2003 and an utterly implausible 2.43 in 1952. No serious scholar credits the latter figure; most would put the ratio somewhere between 1 and 1.2.

To help resolve this puzzle, Heston turns to some revised estimates of output and prices for China prepared by scholars Angus Maddison and Harry Wu. Maddison-Wu have re-estimated China's GDP growth rates downwards from 9.6 per cent per year to 7.9 per cent (for reasons given in Heston's paper). Heston also assumes that in 1952 India's and China's per capita GDP were equal at PPP prices, that is, the ratio was unity, which is within the independently estimated plausible range of 1 to 1.2 noted above. Armed with these adjustments Heston arrives at a much more plausible time series of estimates for the ratio of India's per capita GDP to China's (both PPP-adjusted). Table 31.2 presents the comparisons.

Table 31.2

Ratios of India/China Per Capita GDP at PPP Prices

	Penn World Tables 6.2	*Maddison–Wu Estimates*
1952	2.43	1.00
1978	1.97	0.91
1990	1.13	0.69
2003	0.60	0.42

Source: Heston (2007).

What all this says to me is that the comparison of GDP and growth across countries at PPP prices is a tricky business. So also are such comparisons done at official currency exchange rates. Both types of data have value and relevance—you just need to be very careful when to apply which type for what purpose!

I hope these titbits provide food for thought.

* Barry Eichengreen (2007). "The Cautious Case for Capital Flows", *mimeo.*, paper presented at NIPFP-DEA Research Conference, December 4-5, New Delhi.

** Barry Bosworth, Susan Collins and Aaron Flaaen (2007). "Trading with Asia's Giants", *mimeo.*, paper presented at ICRIER India, China and Global Economy Conference, December 6-7, New Delhi.

*** Alan Heston (2007). "What Can Be Learned About the Economies of China and India from the Results of Purchasing Power Comparisons?" paper presented at ICRIER India, China and Global Economy Conference, December 6-7, New Delhi.

Business Standard, December 13, 2007.

32 A Few Good Men

Years ago, on occasions when our Republic had narrowly escaped some political or policy disaster through sheer luck, finance minister Manmohan Singh would smile wanly and say, "Only God looks after this country!" Perhaps it would have been more accurate to say "God and a few good men..." That's certainly the impression I formed during my 15 years in senior echelons of government: how often a handful of dedicated, talented and hardworking public servants prevented really bad decisions on public policy. Of course, frequently they failed to plug the dykes in the sea of mediocre governance and callous administration. But their success rate was disproportionately high relative to their small numbers and that success was usually achieved against the odds.

No one exemplifies this better than Manmohan Singh himself. Twice in less than two decades he has played the pivotal role in changing the course of India's history. In the early 1990s, as finance minister, he wrought a sea change in India's economic policies, which unleashed the economic dynamism of the last 17 years and led to the country's rise in global economic and political affairs. Now, in the past three months, his tenacious pursuit of the nuclear deal has won the truly historic end of India's 34-year old nuclear and technological isolation. Almost everyone had given up any serious hopes for success a year ago, when the Congress leadership's attempt to force the issue was undercut by its election-fearing, governmental allies and the virulent opposition of the Left. At that time, most of the chatterati, including myself, felt that the publicly humiliated Prime Minister should resign.

Well, speaking for myself, I cover myself in the proverbial sack cloth and ashes, and chant a hundred *mea culpa's*. For Singh didn't just survive and cling to his seemingly powerless office in the well-worn Indian tradition. He kept the deal alive, grasped the political opportunity offered by the Samajwadi Party (SP) after the UP elections and persuaded his UPA colleagues to take the high risk route of a break with the Left and the nail-biting, parliamentary trust vote of late July. And he won...in Parliament in July and in Vienna last week when the Nuclear Suppliers Group agreed to the crucial waiver for India.

Of course, there were many other architects of this enterprise, ranging from political players (including Sonia Gandhi, the Congress political managers, the SP leadership and the US President George Bush with his steadfast support) to the outstanding Indian negotiating team (including Shyam Saran, Shankar Menon, Anil Kakodkar, Ronen Sen, and S. Jaishankar). But when all is said and done, the fact is that this long-sought end to India's nuclear isolation has happened primarily because of two men, Manmohan Singh and George Bush. We owe them gratitude and respect.

Another outstanding public servant demitted office last week. Yaga Venugopal Reddy ended his five-year term as Governor of the RBI and went home to Hyderabad. His contributions were enormous, though under-rated, thanks to his weakness in public relations and the lack of consistent support from a finance ministry with imperfect mastery over sound macroeconomic policy. Courage, independence and foresight were the hallmarks of Reddy's stewardship of the RBI. It took a lot of courage to extend effective regulatory oversight over the giant, politically powerful non-bank financial companies, such as Peerless and Sahara. He achieved substantially more than his predecessors. Similarly with the urban cooperative banks (UCBs) under Reddy the RBI concluded memoranda of understanding with 19 state governments, accounting for over 90 per cent of UCBs. It is also perhaps no coincidence that there was no significant bank failure on his watch and the RBI successfully phased in Basle II norms for capital adequacy across the banking industry.

It took foresight to anticipate the possible perils of explosive bank lending to retail customers and for real estate. From early in Reddy's term, the RBI tightened prudential norms in these areas. He sensed the dangers from exuberant foreign investment in real estate and advocated caution long before the bubbles had built up. Years before most people, Reddy foresaw the serious macroeconomic management challenges posed by the unprecedented acceleration in India's growth and the associated, extraordinary surge in foreign capital inflows. The two big, linked challenges were how to manage the exchange rate and how to calibrate monetary policy. On these big issues, Reddy's RBI made the correct strategic choices. Despite plenty of faulty advice from some commentators, it chose to contain the real appreciation of the rupee through a determined policy of sterilised forex intervention through sales of government securities (via MSS), operations of the liquidity adjustment facility and occasional recourse to CRR increases, combined with a calibrated liberalisation of capital outflows. This effective containment of real appreciation (except in spring/summer of 2007) was the key factor propelling rapid growth of India's exports of goods and services and shielding domestic tradable production from a major, temporary bout of currency overvaluation.

On monetary policy, Reddy began a gradual programme of tightening liquidity conditions right from 2004 and sustained it in the face of both explicit and implicit opposition from the finance ministry, though perhaps less strongly than he would have preferred. After the global commodity price shock of spring 2008 it has become fashionable in some quarters to criticise the RBI and Reddy for "falling behind the curve" in monetary tightening. Some of the same latter-day critics were among those opposing RBI earlier tightening initiatives! The simple fact is that no politically feasible degree of monetary restraint during the go-go years of 2004-2007could have pre-empted the commodity price shock that hit India in March 2008.

Reddy's conduct of monetary and exchange rate management was complicated by a shrill anti-RBI campaign mounted (with governmental encouragement, some claim) by a few columnists with insufficient grasp of modern central banking and even less of common courtesy. Fortunately, Reddy was not deflected from his chosen path by either these diatribes or the rumblings from the finance ministry, except perhaps in spring 2007.One thing is for sure: no one accused Venu Reddy of undermining the autonomy and independence of the RBI!

Let me end by distributing a few personal awards for performance in 2004-2008:

"Most visionary statecraft" goes to Prime Minister Manmohan Singh.

"Best Economic Policymaker" is won by Y. Venugopal Reddy.

"India's best foreign friend" goes to US President George Bush.

"Politician with the worst economics and politics" is won by Prakash Karat.

Business Standard, September 11, 2008.

33 The Audacity of Hope

On Tuesday, November 4, 2008 a miracle happened. America, which had enslaved black people for centuries (till the Emancipation of 1863) and then subjugated and segregated them for another 100 years, elected an African-American as its President. It was an astonishing landmark event in the socio-political history of not just the US but the entire world. It rekindled hopes for renewal and recommitment to the American (and universal) ideals of freedom, equality and democracy. For those of us "urban, anglicised Indians" who had spent much of our early adulthood in America as graduate students and then young professionals, it was a moment resonant with our personal trajectories and memories.

Forty years ago, when my wife and I were graduate students in the Boston area, America was a vibrant, open society, so refreshingly different from the ossified, class-ridden and (then) increasingly racist Britain from whence we had arrived to do further studies. Three powerful movements were churning the social and political fabric of America. First, the civil rights movement, led by Martin Luther King, was going strong and had helped win major legislative victories on voter rights and other issues as part of the "Great Society" reforms of Lyndon Johnson (a hugely underestimated reforming president). Second, the women's movement for social and economic equality was gathering momentum, despite fringe distractions of bra-burning and other antics. Third, the popular opposition to the Vietnam war was reaching a crescendo and, in the wake of the famous Tet offensive of February 1968, was to impel LBJ from seeking re-election. To foreign students like us, the power of popular protest and progressive social movements was both evident and uplifting. Anything seemed possible in this vibrant democracy.

As it turned out, 1968 was also a year for profound disappointments. The shocking assassinations of Dr. King and Robert Kennedy stunned America and the world, and weakened the momentum of the civil rights movement. Kennedy's killing helped rent the Democratic party asunder and contributed to the November victory of Richard Nixon on a conservative platform, deliberately designed to capitalise on the southern white backlash to the civil rights advances of the Kennedy-Johnson years. This strategy swung the southern states into the Republican fold for the next four decades, and ensured that 28 of the next 40 years would see a Republican president in the White House. The Vietnam war dragged on for another seven bloody years as Nixon and Kissinger deliberately widened the scope of the conflict, and the scale and intensity of the bombing.

In the years that followed we watched, with much fascination and some trepidation, the ebb and flow of conservative and liberal ideas and policies in America (by 1982 our vantage point had shifted to Delhi): the brief, liberal, internationalist interlude of Jimmy Carter's presidency; followed by the potent combination of a strident free market ideology and a muscular foreign policy during the Reagan-Bush (Sr.) years; and then the resurrection of a more inclusive social contract by Bill Clinton within an economic framework of fiscal prudence and strong economic growth in the 1990s. Throughout the quarter century after Nixon the vitality of American politics, society and culture remained a source of inspiration for those of us who had studied and worked there in our youth.

The Bush-Cheney-Rumsfeld actions post-9/11 changed all that. The initial US military response against the Al Qaeda and Taliban in Afghanistan was anticipated and understandable (though one cringed when Rumsfeld crowed in his press briefings: "We are not running out of bombing targets, Afghanistan is"). The gratuitous invasion of Iraq was a very different matter. It killed and maimed hundreds of thousands of civilians, made millions of people into homeless, stateless refugees, shredded the social and administrative fabric of the society...and all for no good discernible reason. In Afghanistan a successful military retribution against the terrorist perpetrators of 9/11 became transformed, over time, into a programme of officially sanctioned torture and degradation (remember Abu Ghraib?), "extraordinary rendition" and a seemingly generalised crusade against Islam. At home in the US, the draconian provisions of the 2001 Patriot Act shredded much of the civil liberties and rule of law that generations of Americans had taken for granted. Domestic surveillance of ordinary citizens by hugely powerful and well-equipped intelligence agencies became an accepted reality. Detention of "terror suspects", without due process of law, was sanctioned (the Guantanamo prison is six years old). And heaven help you if you were brown, bearded, with a Muslim name and deemed to be acting suspiciously. This was not the American dream that had drawn millions of immigrants to the country and inspired many millions more with the ideals of freedom, equality before the law and democracy.

Barack Obama's election is a truly historic watershed. As Tom Friedman has written, it ended the 150 year old Civil War in America. On election night the TV network cameras focused on the euphoria of African Americans all over the country from Chicago, to Harlem, to Atlanta. In doing so they may have missed the larger point: Obama's victory brought joy to the majority of *all* Americans, not to mention hundreds of millions across Europe, Asia, and Africa. Obama won not because he got 95 per cent of the black vote and 66 per cent of the Latinos, but because he received 43 per cent of the white vote, the same share won by the last three white Democratic presidential candidates: Clinton, Gore and Kerry. He won because he was a thoughtful, charismatic and enormously skillful candidate who offered a serious and consistent alternative to the Bush-Cheney doctrines; and who happened to be black. He won because in him Americans saw a return to the founding ideals of their nation. It was a victory of hope over fear.

Obama's election will not, by itself, solve the gravest economic and financial crisis since 1930. It will not end the war in Iraq overnight or revert American civil liberties immediately to the pre-2001 status. Or defuse the international hotspots of Pakistan, Iran, and the Middle East. Or provide instant solutions to climate change, energy scarcity and other pressing, planetary problems. But what it will do, indeed has done, is provide real hope that the world's most powerful country will approach these profound problems in a serious, consultative, multilateral way. In international politics there are no cast iron guarantees. But we can hope. Yes, we can.

Business Standard, November 13, 2008.